CONFEDERATES

Killed In Action

AT

GETTYSBURG

Gregory A. Coco

Thomas Publications
Gettysburg, PA 17325

ISBN-1-57747-064-8

LCC#00-91473

Cover design by Ryan C. Stouch

Battleflag sketch by John S. Heiser

Photographs of the flags of the 3rd and 49th Georgia
courtesy of Dorothy Olson, Georgia State Capitol
Museum.

Photograph of Confederate soldier courtesy of Bill and
Brendan Synnamon.

Confederate belt plate courtesy of George Gilpin.

(alg)

DEDICATION

This book is dedicated to the memory of
Lieutenant William Robert Gaylard,
Company I, 3rd North Carolina Infantry, C.S.A.,
a casualty of war.

CONTENTS

Casualties of July 3, 1863

PREFACE

In 1865, when confronted with the enormous number of graves still dotting the Gettysburg battlefield embracing the corpses of what were once living men, a visitor was overwhelmed by the sad reality that every one of those men "had his history." Two years earlier this same feeling occurred to volunteer nurse Sophronia Bucklin. As she viewed the recent carnage, and the crude and often remote burials, Bucklin thought: "Every grave [has] its history, and thousands were there."

And it is still the only proper way to think of these fallen men. Every soldier who filled a grave at Gettysburg, no matter what his rank or background or cause, possessed a personal story, of loves, of interests, of hopes and dreams. For us today, it should be a priority not to reduce them to mere numbers, or "casualties." This belief has been my motivation over the years as I researched and wrote individual accounts of over 200 Gettysburg fatalities. Granted, the figure is small, considering that nearly 10,500 combatants were killed or mortally wounded in the great battle. But detailed stories of those deaths have never been easy to find.

The first time I explored this theme was in 1990, with the publication of *Wasted Valor*, a book about the Confederates who died at Gettysburg. In one chapter, entitled "A Fearful Verification," I tried to document the last moments of 50 Southerners who had lost their lives fighting in Pennsylvania. I found then, as later, that specific material on men "killed in action" is quite difficult to uncover. There are thousands upon thousands of available sources on the battle itself, but most of it is of a general nature. Even when a comrade makes note of a friend's death, more often than not, a sentence or two suffices to tell that, and nothing more. After *Wasted Valor* came out, I learned from many who bought the book that they particularly enjoyed these personal accounts.

Therefore, in 1992, Thomas Publications released *Killed In Action*, a book which followed the final moments of 100 Union soldiers who died as a result of the Battle of Gettysburg. (The title, of course, was not meant to be taken literally, as some of the soldiers had been "mortally wounded" and had not died immediately). It, too, received many favorable comments, and spurred on this latest effort. In the present study, I even up the score by adding to the list 50 more narratives of Confederates who sucumed to the fighting in the Gettysburg Campaign. So now both sides, the Blue and the Gray, are evenly represented. And I hope by learning how these few died, we can come to acknowledge the difficult sacrifices all good men made for their country's sake—and understand that their beliefs were honest and true, no matter which nation they fought for. If this result is achieved, then the purpose for writing these three books is happily fulfilled.

ACKNOWLEDGMENTS

It is often said that no project like this can be completed without generous help. That certainly is the case here, so I would like to thank the following friends and acquaintances for their assistance and support over the last few months as I worked to finish this project. They are: Cindy L. Small, Dean S. Thomas, Sally Thomas, Jim Thomas, Gary Adelman, Andy DeCusati, Kay Stockton, Ryan C. Stouch, Steve Hollingshead, John Heiser, Scott Hartwig, Matt Atkinson, Kathy Harrison, David Wynn Vaughan, Terry Winchel, Pat, Chet, Sam and Wes Small, Charlie W. Clark, Thomas B. Ray, Curt Johnson, Tim Smith (PA), Tim Smith (VA), Dorothy Olson, Bob Gale, Paul Sledzik, Bill and Brendan Synnamon, Eileen F. Conklin, John E. Calvin, and last but not least, Joe "Law Dog" Rankin.

Special acknowledgement is given to Addie Lee Gaylord, for keeping alive the deeds of her Confederate ancestor, Lt. William R. Gaylard. In times like these, when assaults on the memories of Confederate soldiers grow stronger each day, I wish there were many more like her.

"Nothing symbolizes the modern age's difficulty in understanding [our history], more than the easy moral outrage that encourages the present to simplify the past in order to condemn it."

Gregory A. Coco
Aspers, PA
December 9, 2000

INTRODUCTION

Gettysburg! Name instinct with so many tears, with so much mourning, with those sobs, which tear their way from the human heart as lava makes its way from the womb of the volcano. There are words in the world's history whose very sound is like a sigh or a groan; places which are branded "accursed" by the moaning lips of mothers, wives, sisters and orphans. Among them none is more gloomier or instinct with a more nameless horror than the once insignificant village of Gettysburg. It has been called "pivotal Gettysburg," though it savors of a paradox, because there was neither victor nor vanquished, only the culmination.

Written by a veteran, the above words, read long after the event they describe, still have the power to affect our emotions. Yet for the participants of the times, those few dreary sentences would have meant more than just another piece of dramatic prose. To the hundreds of thousands of parents and other close family members who lost sons and brothers and husbands in the violence and danger of the Civil War years, this language would have cut to the heart of their very nature. For no other event in American history had ever come close to duplicating the suffering of those four grim years, where blood flowed out like water, and where death stalked the land in all its ghastly forms. And nothing else since those days, has accumulated for our country such a great toll of anguish.

The "culmination" spoken of, meant that Gettysburg, for war casualties, was the peak and the climax of bitter pain for a nation drowning in its own sorrow and misfortune. At Gettysburg, the roster of deaths rose to a summit unprecedented in any of the thousands of battles fought between 1861 and 1865. The dates and places of these battles became curses to the living, left without those they loved, cherished, and needed. Therefore, Gettysburg with its 10,500 lives expended, was at the apex of the great calamity.

The stories presented here are an attempt to balance the glory and excitement of war with the sadness and loss attendant. The accounts are interesting in their own right, whether the reader feels compassion for the victims or not. But if we are able to reflect further upon the unique personal tragedies within these pages, and remember that the fifty soldiers here represented are not even a minute fraction of the 620,000 men who died in the war, then perhaps the enormity of the terrible struggles of the 1860s will become more real to us in this age of peace and prosperity.

The epitome of the "culmination," this pitiless desolation of the heart, could describe many who lost a loved one at Gettysburg. But few could claim a distinction so woeful as that of Margery Rogers Clark, a Southern woman from Calhoun County, Mississippi.

Calhoun was almost as rural a place as could be found in Mississippi; in fact, the largest town today probably cannot boast more than 3000 people. Margery B. Rogers Clark moved from Alabama sometime around 1850, to the fertile lands of north central Mississippi. There, among the "gentle rolling hills," Margery, with her husband Thomas, and their sons, Jonathan, Albert Henry, and Isaac, began a new life. Daily existence on a farm was not always easy, but the days at least went on peacefully, as Margery and Thomas' family grew and prospered in the years preceding the presidential election of 1860.

Following Lincoln's victory, however, everyday life in the South began to change radically. With the secession of South Carolina on December 20, 1860, events began to spiral rapidly out of control. How Margery took this astounding news, and the news that Mississippi would become the second state to leave the Union, on January 9, 1861, is unknown. Within a few months it was too late for anyone to look back, for the firing on Fort Sumter in April spelled the end of the normal world that the Clark family had known for so long.

By November, Mississippi, then part of the fledgling Confederate States of America, was deep in the throes of a military buildup. Margery's husband, Thomas Goode Clark, was not immune to the war's patriotic lure. During this time when men were enlisting at the drop of a hat, Thomas wrote to Margery saying, "...I came out for the purpose of doing my country all that was in my power and I am determined to do my duty as far as I can...." What Margery thought of all this excitement and upheaval is impossible to know, but when Thomas, and her sons Jonathan and Albert Henry, ages 21 and 18, met with others in Sarepta, Mississippi, in November 1861 to form a company, surely that decision caused her to reflect on what the future might hold. The far-off hostilities along the eastern seaboard were but a harbinger of what lay ahead, and when families in Mississippi began to arm and ready themselves, a disquieting feeling must have come over Margery and many other caring wives and mothers in the Deep South.

But fortunately, the first enlistment of Thomas and his sons did not amount to much, mainly because it lasted only 60 days and was a "local defense" measure only, so Margery would have had little cause to worry. In April 1862 however, a new company was mustered at Sarepta; it became Company F, 42nd Mississippi Infantry, and Thomas Clark was elected captain. Albert Henry wrote to a friend during this period, and his words no doubt reflected the mood of many untested Confederate soldiers: "The time has come when we will have to fight or be conquered and I believe it is the firm resolution of every true Southerner to never be whipped.... I tell you Bill, I am for Southern rights, right or wrong. Let me go!"

By July, Clark's company and the balance of the 42nd had made the long trip to Virginia, where they eventually became part of Robert E. Lee's Army of Northern Virginia. In early November 1862 the regiment was joined by the 2nd and 11th Mississippi, and the 55th North Carolina, forming a new brigade under General Joseph R. Davis. This brigade was soon ordered to North Carolina where they spent the winter of 1862-1863. From the letters the family preserved, it is apparent that Thomas was longing to return to Calhoun County. One day when he heard a preacher in camp telling the men that they would all be home in time to plant a spring crop, Thomas confided in a letter to Margery that, "...I am afraid he will miss it just a little and the war will turn out to be the most barbarous war that history could ever tell."

Meanwhile Margery Clark, and others like her with family members at the front, begin to amass their own problems. Yankee incursions into northern Mississippi, with their ensuing depredations throughout the countryside, placed added burdens on lives already filled with unusual difficulties. Worry about enemy soldiers rampaging in Mississippi affected the men of the 42nd and other units; it hurt morale, and caused many applications for leave and even some desertions. When Thomas heard the chilling stories of his people being "treated badly," and then learned that his fourteen-year-old son Isaac had run off to join the army, his requests for a furlough became more urgent. As the new year rolled around, Thomas was still committed to his duty as a soldier, but not an hour passed when he did not wish to see Margery. "Oh, that I could be there only one day," he wrote her, "but when I think of home I resolve to fight on through the war with more firmness than ever, looking forward to the close of our troubles when we shall meet to part no more."

Although the 42nd Mississippi had so far seen no real action, by the spring of 1863 Captain Clark was sure his men were ready for battle. Proud of his unit, he told Margery that Company F could be counted on, and that they "will do themselves honor." He said too, as always, that he wished the "cruel war will soon be over."

Finally, in April 1863, Thomas Clark received a long-awaited leave of absence. During a portion of the time the captain was gone, Jonathan and Albert Henry and the rest of Davis' Brigade skirmished with the Federals in "regular picket fighting for 23 days," near Suffolk, Virginia. It was a difficult period for the brigade. Jonathan described their hard experiences in a letter to his mother, telling her that the enemy had got the best of them, and the retreat from Suffolk was pretty rough. "I have never seen so many men broken down in my life—thousands lying along the roadside. Far better to be home but never mind that.... I am willing to do all I can to save our country.... My country needs me and I will stay here."

Later, in the first weeks of May, Captain Clark returned from his Mississippi furlough. A month or so went by, and in early June, Thomas sent a letter to Margery, explaining that "[e]vidently something is about, but I can't tell what. Some think...General Lee will make a forward move and will probably go into Maryland but...it is impossible for us to know until we receive orders."

A movement had indeed begun, but the destination was farther north, and into Pennsylvania. During this campaign, the 42nd Mississippi of Davis' Brigade was assigned to Lee's Third Corps, with the division of General Henry Heth. This put them in the forefront of the combat that started just west of Gettysburg on Wednesday, July 1, 1863. It was around 9:30 a.m. that Davis' Brigade, lacking one regi-

(CWC)

Captain Thomas Clark (left) was one of the first Confederates killed at Gettysburg. He was soon joined in death by two of his sons, Albert (center) and Jonathan (right).

ment, began its advance eastward toward Union troops posted along McPherson's Ridge. The brigade was deployed north of the Chambersburg Pike and on across a railroad bed, with the 42nd holding the right flank nearest to the road.

In their first real battle, sometime during that day, and somewhere in that vicinity, Captain Thomas Clark and his son Albert Henry fell dead, "killed in action" at Gettysburg. No one knows positively, but it appears from family sources that Jonathan survived the first day's fighting. If so, then when a Confederate victory was assured on July 1, it is likely that he returned that evening to the fields along the pike, and on or adjacent to the Edward McPherson farm, and prepared a grave for his father, his brother, and for another officer of the regiment, Captain James H. Gaston of Company G. However, a nephew of Captain Clark, Archibald T. Roane, wrote many years after the war that the burial might have been undertaken by Albert Henry, not Jonathan, or by Sergeant James M. Duncan of Company F. The exact details, of course, as in many of these cases, may never be ascertained.

If Jonathan did indeed become the family gravedigger, than none can pretend to imagine what that sad duty meant to the young man. His closest companions in the army and in the world were gone. And, he was a thousand miles from his mother's side, laden with news that when disclosed, would destroy Margery Clark's world forever. Furthermore, it was impossible for Jonathan to foresee that the chance to deliver that terrible message would never come, for his own death was only hours away. According to military records in the Clark ancestry, Jonathan died with many of his comrades of Davis' Brigade on the afternoon of July 3, in an attack on Cemetery Ridge in what is now called the "Pickett-Pettigrew Charge."

Weeks afterward, Margery Clark read the reports of the 42nd Mississippi's shocking losses at Gettysburg. Out of 575 men present during the battle, 75 were killed, and another 190 wounded. At least three of those deaths were very dear to her: Thomas Goode, Jonathan, and Albert Henry. A granddaughter later wrote about Margery's triple tragedy:

> When she received the news she cried and shouted all night long. The greatest Sorrow that came into the life of Grandmother Clark was that of giving up her husband and two sons in the cause of freedom. They...sleep today under the sod of that historic battlefield.

There are two conflicting stories concerning the final disposition of the three Clark bodies that have come down to us through the years. The first, as you just read, states that their remains were thought to still be buried at Gettysburg. Another source in the family record indicates that the men were "removed to the Hollywood Cemetery in Richmond, Virginia." It is now known that both of these views may have some validity.

Regarding at least two of the Clark burials at Gettysburg, there can be no doubt. It is known positively that Thomas and one of his sons, probably Albert Henry, were interred on the first day's field along with the aforementioned Captain Gaston. The reason these facts are undisputed is due to a short paragraph which appeared in a local newspaper on May 29, 1888. It read:

> Relic—Mrs. Clayton Hoke, some time ago, found, near the Chambersburg turnpike, a piece of white pine board, about nine inches square, marked as follows:

>
>
> Capt. J. M. Gaston.
> Capt. T. G. Clark and son.
> 42d Miss. Vols.
> Killed July 1st, 1863.
>
>

> The marking is very distinct; looks as if the letters had been cut with a sharp-bladed knife, and the lines afterwards followed by a pointed piece of iron or course wire heated. This notice of the relic is made with the hope that it may meet the eye of someone directly interested.

The existence of this headboard proves beyond a doubt that at least two of the Clarks received a better than average burial. This was something that Jonathan, if he was actually the son killed in "Pickett's Charge," certainly did not receive. Regarding all of this, a mystery, or a problem, now presents itself. If Captain Gaston, Thomas Clark, "and son" once had such a conspicuous gravesite, then where are their remains today? It is a compelling fact that when Gettysburg physician John W. C. O'Neal made surveys of identified Confederates buried on the battlefield in the early fall of 1863, October 1864, and May 1866, he failed to make note of such a well-defined grave.

How had this happened? Had O'Neal simply missed the spot during his three visits, or was the marker already dislocated from the burial mound when he made his observations?

Years later, in 1870, former Gettysburg resident Dr. Rufus B. Weaver was given a contract from several "Southern Ladies Memorial Societies" to remove the Confederate dead from the old battleground, and deliver them to various city cemeteries in the South. In 1872 and 1873 Weaver completed six shipments to Hollywood Cemetery in Richmond, Virginia, totaling 2935 remains. Many of these soldiers had been taken from identified graves, yet Captains Gaston and Clark were absent from those transported and reinterred in Virginia. One of Dr. Weaver's lists states that he filled three boxes with the bones of 34 men of Generals Hill and Early's commands, from "McPherson's field to [the] rear of Seminary Ridge or more particularly back of the Rail Road cut." This location is contiguous to where the 42nd Mississippi fought, but Weaver does not identify any of those bodies. Therefore, despite a perfectly noticeable grave, we can now accept that Gaston, Clark, and his son, if they were found at all, made the trip to Richmond as "unknowns." As for Jonathan, assuming that he fell on July 3, his corpse was surely buried by the enemy in one of the shallow trenches in the fields along the Emmitsburg Road or near Cemetery Ridge, together with hundreds of comrades from Pettigrew's and Pickett's Divisions. These Southerners were never identified, but most were exhumed and made the journey to Hollywood Cemetery between 1872 and 73.

The end of this story has a curious twist. Remember how the headboard over the Gaston/Clark grave was found 25 years after the battle by the wife of Clayton Hoke? Well, the old "pine board" eventually took on a life of its own. After serving for a short time "in memory" of the three brave Mississippians, the nine inch wide artifact made its way from the possession of Mrs. Hoke to one of the largest collections of Civil War relics ever assembled.

John W. C. O'Neal and Rufus B. Weaver. The two physicians who saved the identities of over a thousand Confederates who died at Gettysburg. (achs)

This happened when Chicago businessman Charles F. Gunther, who had a passion for accumulating memorabilia from the war, decided to open a museum to house his historic acquisitions. For the centerpiece of his great collection, he chose one of the most impressive antiques of all, the infamous Libby Prison in Richmond, Virginia. By late summer of 1889 the old Confederate structure had been moved to Chicago and rebuilt, brick by brick, nearly a million in all. When Gunther's museum opened later that year, nine huge rooms of the former "Rebel" military prison went on view. The museum also contained thousands of items used by Northerners and Southerners between 1861-1865, and yes, one of the attractions was a small, rough, weather-beaten board, "its edges and corners...rounded by time," that had crowned the Gettysburg grave of Captain Gaston and the Clarks.

Nothing lasts forever, not even memories. This is the one certainty of the universe. Observe how the Civil War itself is fast becoming just a footnote of our history. The bodies of the dead from that war are mostly forgotten. Brave and true men like Thomas Clark and his young sons, the great and worthy sacrifices of that once important time, are long gone. Even their bones, wherever they lie, have by now surely crumbled into dust. Mr. Gunther's enormous stone and brick museum, too, has passed away: you would be hard pressed to find a Chicagoan today who has ever heard of it. The whereabouts of the tiny wooden board is unknown, if it still exists, like most of the other wonderful pieces that once adorned the walls of old "Libby."

But in all this regret there remains one bright spot, and it shines up from Bruce, Mississippi, in Calhoun County. Living there is a gentleman who is directly related to Captain Thomas Goode Clark. His name is Charlie W. Clark, and like others throughout the South, he is dedicated to keeping the memory of his ancestors alive. The headboard is often on his mind; to Charlie Clark, finding it would be a treasure beyond any riches he could ever attain. And just this year Charlie wrote down the story of his Confederate relatives. In the last section he commented on why he still cares, saying: "The family continues the search for this little marker, which is so representative of the tragic loss sustained by families on both sides of the conflict."

The word "loss" in Charlie's statement describes what this book is essentially about. And if Margery Clark were here to read the stories that follow, I trust she would be pleased at this frail attempt to memorialize a few of the dead of her beloved Southland.

> And the dead thus meet the dead,
> While the living o'er them weep;
> And the men whom Lee and Stonewall led,
> And the hearts that once together bled,
> Together still shall sleep.

The Casualties Of Day One: July 1, 1863

THREE TOGETHER TO THE END

Corporal Charles L. Humphreys,
Co. E, 2nd Mississippi Infantry
Davis' Brigade, Heth's Division, Hill's Corps

The Gettysburg experiences of a trio of wounded Mississippians, Samuel W. Hankins, William K. Weemes, and Charles L. Humphreys, represent a lesson on the cruelties of war, and an example of how luck and simple chance manipulate the fortunes and fate of humankind.

While not yet true veterans, for they had seen little combat, these three comrades were thrown together for two weeks by cruel circumstances beyond their control. They all shared what could be described as a bad dream from which only two would awake. Yet their suffering and neglect was but a small sample of a pattern, set and followed by thousands like them through four years of bloody civil war.

It all began on the morning of July 1, west of Gettysburg. This was the first actual battle for General Joseph Davis' Brigade, yet his troops fiercely attacked General Lysander Cutler's Federal regiments north of a railroad bed paralleling the Chambersburg Pike. The resulting fighting was close and severe, and Davis' Mississippi and North Carolina troops quickly got a taste of what it was like to be real soldiers. One participant saw the action there almost poetically, saying that a "vicious snarl rose and fell as Hill's brigades were ground to powder in [the battle's] bloody jaws."

Company E entered the fray with 46 men; two days later it mustered only two. Private Samuel Hankins was one of those "ground to powder" on that hard Wednesday morn. He was shot near one of the railroad "cuts," and the Yankee minie ball inflicted a painful injury to his instep, breaking the bones of the foot, and then lodging against the heel leader. Hankins was carried back a short distance where he encountered four other members of Company E, Weemes, Humphreys, Wilson and Keys. Wilson died shortly afterwards, and as Keys was able to walk, he moved on to the rear. This left only three.

Soon, Hankins' foot began to cramp. "Never have I felt such agony," he recalled, but his screams brought help. An old schoolmate, Jim Schell of the 11th Mississippi, came to his aid. He called a surgeon who removed the ball, using a knife, said Hankins, which was probably "kept on hand for sharpening slate pencils."

"Jim dressed my wound nicely," related Hankins, "also that of Weems, who was shot through the thigh, and of Humphreys, who was shot in the right side and liver.... Then an old oilcloth was spread on the ground by some of the field nurses, and we were all three placed on it with a rock each for a pillow, Humphreys being placed in the center."

For seventeen days the men never really left that oilcloth, which was located on or very near the first day's battleground. Strangely, they were never transported to an established field hospital, when the nearest was just a few miles away. Hankins mentioned that their "wounds were redressed once by the surgeon before General Lee began falling back on the fourth day..." This might indicate the presence of roving medical personnel tending to men who were not yet removed to regular military medical facilities.

When Lee's army did start its retreat, Hankins said that any wounded "that were able to sit upright in ambulances," would be returned to Virginia. "Weem[e]s, Humphreys, and I were not taken," he reported, "I begged hard to go.... The surgeon then told me that I could not travel,.... All the time that he was saying this to me Weems and Humphreys were begging me to remain with them, so I consented."

According to Hankins, thirty minutes after the Confederate rear guard was out of sight, Union dismounted cavalry appeared and began collecting and destroying discarded muskets. He declared:

No attention whatever had we [from the Yankees]...until the evening of July 18.... If the good Lord had not sent us rain every day, we would have perished for water. There happened to be a few small gullies that would hold a canteen or two of water some six or eight spaces from us to which Weems and I would crawl the best we could, fill our canteens, then crawl back to our oilcloth and proceed to dress our wounds, using the same bandages, but washing them each day. I would assist Weems with his wound, he in turn would assist me, and we both together would dress the wound of Humphreys.

The only food received was on "two occasions when a passing soldier dropped us some hard-tack and a small piece of salt pork[,] the latter had to be eaten uncooked."

While the long and dreary days drifted by, the three companions watched as clean-up details broke up old weapons and hauled usable equipment to the railroad depot in Gettysburg. Yet no person came to their aid. "[The Yankees] threw a few shovels of dirt over our dead," noted Hankins. "The horses they

17

dragged up into long rows, attempting to burn them. They failed in this, but raised a fearful stench." But with all this activity, no one lifted a finger to help. Finally, on July 15, after having spent more than two weeks on the ground, with no covering, very little food to eat, and only polluted water to drink, Charley Humphreys' bodily functions gave up and shut down. He died, lying there, still warmed by the friends who never left his side. "No sooner had breath left his body," observed Private Hankins, "than two soldiers dragged him by the heels from between us to the front some six or eight feet, where they covered him slightly with shovels of dirt."

Three days later, on the eighteenth according to Hankins, "a Dutchman with his dump cart halted in front of us and ordered Weems and myself to crawl in, 'and be damned quick about it,' which we did as soon as we could gather our effects together.... Our Dutchman soon had us jolting over a stony field. As the sun was setting he dumped us out by the side of the railroad track along with about two hundred and fifty other wounded who had been gathered up during the day."

That night, Weemes and Hankins began their long journey to a Northern prison camp. As the train departed the Gettysburg station, something valuable sat snugly inside the greasy haversack of Sam Hankins. It was a gold ring and pocketbook that had once belonged to a friend and fellow soldier,—Corporal Charles L. Humphreys, now deceased, but never deserted.

A BROTHER'S LOVE

Private Benjamin H. Stone,
Page's Virginia Battery
Carter's Battalion, Rodes' Division, Ewell's Corps

In the majority of Civil War battles, the greatest losses generally occurred in the infantry regiments; the cavalry and artillery mostly escaped with lighter casualties. On the Confederate side in the Battle of Gettysburg, the Southern battery with the highest percentage of losses, (34.2%), was Captain Richard Page's Virginia Battery, also known as the Morris, Louisa, or Davis Artillery. This unit was organized on August 19, 1861, in Louisa County, and its first captain was Lewis M. Coleman.

Although the battery participated in many of the campaigns of the Army of Northern Virginia, from the Seven Days' Battles to Appomattox, it fought its most damaging action on July 1, 1863, just below Oak Hill a mile northwest of Gettysburg. On that unforgettable day, it took into combat 114 officers and men and about 53 horses. According to the battalion commander, Lieutenant Colonel Thomas H. Carter, Page's, along with another battery, were ordered to move to a position to support Colonel Edward O'Neal's Alabama Brigade then in contact with Federal forces on Oak Ridge and along the Mummasburg Road. At that time, O'Neal's men were being hit hard on their front and flank by both Union First Corps and Eleventh Corps troops. Captain Page ordered "action front," and his crews opened fire on the enemy with four 12-pounder Napoleon guns "from a point at the foot of [Oak Hill]," firing a total of 215 rounds. During that interval, Page's artillerymen and horses suffered greatly from "a very destructive oblique fire," which killed and incapacitated 17 animals, and 39 men.

> Then shook the hills, with thunder riven,
> Then rushed the steed to battle driven,
> And louder than the bolts of heaven,
> Far flashed the red artillery.

Of the seven cannoneers killed or mortally wounded in this action, one soldier suffered a particularly harsh end. He was Private Ben Stone, who was "wounded to death with twenty-three musket balls in his body." It is not known if the 23 balls came from infantry musketry, or from an exploding case shot or shrapnel shell, as both were being fired at the battery on that day.

Yet one thing is certain. During a lull in the fighting Benjamin was given a decent burial by his older brother, Spottswood Stone. In 1866 his grave location was entered into the record book of Gettysburg physician, Dr. John W. C. O'Neal. The doctor placed the site at the Elizabeth Hankey farm on the Mummasburg Road. But years later, in 1873, Dr. Rufus B. Weaver, then completing the exhumation of all Confederate dead from the huge battlefield, listed "B. H. Stone" as, "Removed by his brother to Ashland, Hanover Cty Va." A second Weaver entry included the above statement, but added that Stone's remains were packed in a box numbered "184." Dr. Weaver also specifically noted that Benjamin Stone had been buried under a peach tree, north of the farm house of David Schriver, on the same road, and near Hankey's. Both places served as hospitals for General Rodes' Division.

So after the cold fortunes of war sent him to his death, Private Stone received a gift that few Confederates did who died at Gettysburg. His body was carefully interred on the battlefield by a member of his family. Then following the four year conflict, his bones were lifted up and transported home by that same loving brother, to lie wrapped forever, in the Southern soil of his native state.

BATHED IN HIS BLOOD

Captain Campbell T. Iredell,
Co. C, 47th North Carolina Infantry
Pettigrew's Brigade, Heth's Division, Longstreet's Corps

When a soldier dies in battle, it is relatively easy for noncombatants to imagine how that death will affect a mother or father, a loving sister or brother, and the close friends and other relatives of the slain warrior. Yet in our modern society, where peace has reigned for decades, and few of the populace are under arms, the loss in combat of someone known to us, can be as remote as a trip into outer space.

During our Civil War, hundreds of thousands of men died, and literally millions of civilians were closely affected by these casualties. This is readily understood, as the population of the nation was then quite small. But in all of this, there is one factor which is often overlooked by people studying this American conflict. And that is, real grief and personal loss was also felt by the *comrades-in-arms* of those who died in battle, or of wounds and disease. And this sorrow could often be worse for the dead soldier's former companions, than for his civilian acquaintances at home. The years and months spent together marching side by side, eating and sleeping in close proximity, fighting shoulder to shoulder, and sharing hardships, dangers and adventures, within the context of army life, often drew men into a faithful and intimate fraternity like no family on earth.

This concept might be better understood in the story of Captain Iredell's death, and the testimony left by his brotherly companion, Captain Louis G. Young, an *aide-de-camp* to General Pettigrew.

Campbell Tredwell Iredell was born in Wake County in 1836, and was working as a druggist when he enlisted into the Confederate army in 1861. Two years later, and during the first day of the Battle of Gettysburg, he had the misfortune to have "his arm shot off" by cannon fire. This event occurred either in the morning while Pettigrew's Brigade waited to go into action, or later in the afternoon when the brigade engaged Union infantry and artillery near Willoughby's Run. It is obvious from Captain Young's testimony that when Iredell was hit, the wound was thought to be serious but not fatal. Young must have held and comforted his friend for a while, because he stated that his hands were "bathed" in Iredell's "flowing blood."

In time, Captain Iredell was carried to a field hospital of Pettigrew's Brigade two miles northwest of Gettysburg. This facility was located on the north side of the Chambersburg Turnpike at the farm of a man named Charles B. Polly. There, sometime between July 1-3, and probably within the walls of the farmer's brick house, and in the company of many of the wounded of his brigade, Captain Iredell took his last breaths.

Meanwhile Captain Young, who held a position on General Pettigrew's staff, continued to carry out his duties, knowing nothing of the worsening condition of his comrade. But on July 3, just prior to the attack history would forever call the "Pickett-Pettigrew Charge," Young received the dreadful news. And clearly, time never diminished the sadness and hurt he felt that day, for Young wrote these revealing sentiments in 1866, in the first year after a Southern defeat had overturned his world:

> While lying in our position looking at the preparations being made for the grand assault, intelligence was brought me of the death of one of my dearest friends, Captain Campbell T. Iredell, Co. C., 47th N.C. He had lost his right arm by a shell in the first days fight, but his death was totally unexpected, and I cannot express the grief it gave me. —Dear Cam. two long heart-corroding years have passed since then, yet it is an event of to-day.—The memory of the past comes over my soul. Our marches, our bivouacs, our wants, our abundance, our sorrow, our rejoicings, each and all, they were common to us both.
>
> When on that fatal field, thou wast stricken unto death, it was I, whose heart beat proud at thy heroic bearing, it was I, whose hands, in thy support, were bathed in thy flowing blood, —shed a holy sacrifice for liberty. And to-day, upon that blood-washed field, the green grass waves between thy clay and heaven. Sleep Well! —though in a stranger's land—undisturbed by the mighty noise of thousands, who come to commemorate—my defeat, —thy victory. Sleep well! for in this our sorrow-stricken land, there are faithful ones, who daily bend the knee here, while their hearts are resting there, in the grave with thee. And I, not among the least, will cherish the memory of thy manly virtues, until this weak flesh shall sleep its long, last sleep, where our souls shall commune together again in the spirit land.

> Sleep soldier! still in honored rest,
>   Your truth and valor wearing;
>   The bravest are the tenderest,—
>   The loving are the daring.

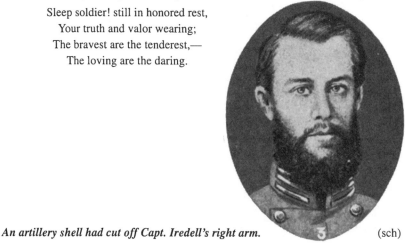

An artillery shell had cut off Capt. Iredell's right arm.   (sch)

When the charge was over, which brought a close to the battle, Captain Young had no opportunity to return to the rear to locate the body of his friend Iredell and prepare a decent burial. At that moment, Young had his own troubles. He had become a casualty of the assault, and was lying helplessly wounded in two places. After being taken to his division's hospital for treatment, Louis Young was placed in an ambulance for the trip back to Virginia. However, on the retreat the wagon train was attacked by Federal cavalry, and the captain became a prisoner-of-war. Therefore, the duty of placing Captain Iredell underground must have fallen to a medical attendant stationed at the Polly farm.

The records of Dr. O'Neal do show a grave for Captain Iredell there, along with six others from Pettigrew's Brigade, and curiously, also from Anderson's Brigade of Hood's Division. By the summer of 1866 however, all the graves on this farm were exhumed or obliterated, except one of a Georgia officer. The postwar lists of removals to cemeteries in North Carolina and Virginia do not contain the name of "C. T. Iredell." This causes one to question the possibility of his and other remains at Mr. Polly's being collected by family members and carried to the South, prior to 1866. Or, the graves might have been simply plowed over. It would be interesting to know, because obviously, according to what we have just read, Captain Young believed in late 1866 that Iredell was still in Pennsylvania, and would be buried there forever.

A SCENE...
WE NEVER WISH TO SEE AGAIN

Unknown captain,
Georgia Infantry,
Ewell's Corps

Following the battle, and before Lee's army departed, nearly 13,000 Confederate wounded remained scattered in and around the Gettysburg area, all sequestered within the various field hospitals set up by the medical corps of both sides. The Union army, in no better condition, had close to 15,000 of its own injured to tend to. And yet these combined figures do not reflect many of the less seriously wounded who were often not counted. The wounds in these makeshift hospitals fit all categories, for men were usually described as having been hurt, "slightly," "badly," or "terribly." But after the fighting ended, the seriousness of the injuries of least two soldiers went far beyond this basic scale. Their critically massive wounds made them unique, and way off any chart.

The first of these remarkable cases was encountered by a nurse, Sister Mary David Salomon, who was originally from Alsace, France. She was a "Daughter of Charity," one of a group which came up from St. Joseph's Convent in Emmitsburg, Maryland, to assist some of the 22,000 wounded left in the wake of the two great armies following their departure. Her plaintive recollection centered on an unnamed soldier who had had both his legs and arms torn off by the explosion of an artillery shell. "I can see him now after all these years," said Sister Mary David, "only the head and trunk of a man as they brought him in and leaned him up against a corner."

This graphic depiction of one so grievously hurt seems unreal, almost made up. In essence, an image like that is just too horrible, and it loses the power to register in the brain of anyone who has not been a spectator to such a scene. And very few people, if any, have ever been an observer in an event similar to the "vast sea of misery" that was Gettysburg in its aftermath.

Sister Mary David Salomon's curt acknowledgement of what was left of a human being probably stemmed from her revulsion at what she had seen that day in a Gettysburg field hospital. The next depiction provides a more lengthy comment on an equally lamentable spectacle— or perhaps both stories focused on the same individual. This second encounter was written by Charles P. Cole, the editor of a Cortland, New York, newspaper, called the *Gazette and Banner*. Cole had traveled to the battlefield at Gettysburg in southern Pennsylvania to find the body of a hometown resident killed there on July 1. He arrived on Monday, July 6, and after completing his intended mission, he decided to visit some sections of the field, and a few of the hospitals.

The first place Cole happened upon was the main edifice of Pennsylvania College, a large white building used as the student dormitory and classrooms when school was in session. The three-story structure had been converted into a Confederate hospital when Cole entered it on his tour. (Only four Daughters of Charity were present that day, caring for over 600 Confederates.) In one of the rooms Cole chanced upon a Mississippi officer, who as a civilian, he had met in New York before the war. That officer was only slightly injured, but nearby, in sharp contrast, was another soldier in much worse condition. Charles Cole explained:

> In the same room we witnessed a scene which was heartrending indeed, and one which we never wish to see again. A young captain in the rebel army from Georgia was lying upon a blanket on the floor, having had both legs and arms shot off in the terrific battle of Wednesday. His features were fine, and his countenance strikingly intellectual. A day or so before the battle he had received a letter from his young wife, but as yet had not read it, and while we were present he asked one of his comrades to open the letter and read it to him, which was done. The letter was filled with assurances of prayers and bless-

23

ings for the Southern army, and urging her husband to fight gallantly for the cause of the South. Alas! he had fought his last fight! A moment after, a surgeon addressed him, saying "Captain, we can do nothing for you; you can live but a short time." Tears rolled down the pale face of the young man, but he had not a hand to wipe them away. We wiped the tears from his eyes and gave him some water, when he looked up, and said, "Thank God, I am going to die beneath the stars and stripes." We could not help turning away and weeping.

After reading Cole's account, (biased or not), which was published in the aforementioned Courtland newspaper on July 16, it seemed appropriate to give this poor "Rebel" captain's story a new and wider audience. At first there was even some hope of providing the officer with an identity, therefore performing a good service in his behalf, and for anyone claiming him as an ancestor. There were many clues. The soldier, according to Cole, was a Georgian wounded on July 1, and there were less than a dozen Georgia regiments in combat that day. Also, his rank and place of death were established. Finally, his injury was a particularly grievous one, and should have been remembered by someone besides Cole. All of these factors gave promise that the young officer's name and unit might be uncovered.

But alas, that has not been the case. Of all the Georgia captains who died as a result of the battle, only two could be verified as having been wounded on the first of July. They were Captains John T. Lane, 4th Georgia Infantry, and Virgil T. Nunnerlly, 13th Georgia Infantry. Both officers were present in regiments which saw action near the college. However, beyond these slim threads, nothing stands out to indicate a possible match. The records tell us that Nunnerlly was "killed" on July 1, and that Lane was "wounded in the left arm," and died on July 25. So as a last resort, the six identified Confederate burials near Pennsylvania College were examined, but none met any of the necessary criteria.

If Mr. Cole got his facts correct and took no literary license, the identity of this young man must remain hidden, too hazy and indistinct, like a shadow, to be known. His injuries were a punishment worse than death, and knowledge of his "self" would at least comfort those who must read of his fate.

HE ACTED VERY BRAVELY

Captain William C. Ousby,
Co. F, 43rd North Carolina Infantry
Daniel's Brigade, Rodes' Division, Ewell's Corps

"Death took the widow's son, and the aged father's staff. The remorseless bullets seemed vulture beaked, and tore alike into hearts throbbing with high hopes...."

So many men in the very prime of life died on both sides at Gettysburg, and correspondingly, on each and every one of more than ten thousand battle grounds of the Civil War.

> And each man had his history; each soldier...had his interest, his loves, his darling hopes, the same as you and I. All were laid down with his life. It was no trifle to him, it was as great a thing to him as it would be to you, thus to be cut off from all things dear in this world, and to drop at once into a vague eternity.... Did they believe in your better world? Whether they did or not, this world was a reality, and dear to them.

It was surely with an honorable frame of mind, and in a spirit of patriotism, that William Clark Ousby, a 28-year-old farmer from Halifax County, chose to volunteer his services in April 1861, only thirteen days following the opening clash at Fort Sumter. "Through trouble, toils, and privations,—not insensible to danger, but braving it,—these men—confronted, for their country's sake, that awful uncertainty."

For Captain Ousby, "that awful uncertainty" had come and gone before, but at Gettysburg, on the first day of fighting, it became reality. Ousby's story serves as a reminder of the terrible suddenness one could become a battlefield casualty. In his case however, faded paper and old ink allow the present to visit the past, where the sadness of William Ousby's separation from his life, can move us all to mourn for the slaughtered hero.

The letter that survived to describe the events comes from another officer of the 43rd North Carolina, Lieutenant Henry A. Macon. In it he notifies James Litchford Ousby of his brother's end:

General Hospital # 4
Richmond, Virginia
July 28th. 1863

Mr. J. L. Ousby
Dear Sir: -

> I take the present opportunity of writing you a few lines to let you hear the particulars of your brother's death. I would have written to you before but was taken sick directly after we crossed this side of the Potomac and have been confined to my bed ever since.
>
> Your brother was killed on the first day of July, that was the first days fight. He was struck by a minney ball in the left breast about fifteen minutes after the battle commenced and died immediately without speaking a word. He acted very bravely and was killed at his post.
>
> I had him buried as good as circumstances would admit, and his name, rank and regiment, cut on a board and put at the head of his grave. He was wrapped in a blanket and put in a bark coffin, this was the best that could be done for him. He had one hundred and nine dollars in his pocket which I have deposited for safe keeping with our cook, [Private Oliver] P. Thrower, also his sword and pistol. I think that it will be necessary for you to come to the regiment as

soon as you can and settle his affairs. If you cannot come now you had better write me word when you can come. I do not know when I shall be able to go back to the regiment. I may get a furlough and if I do I can see you at Halifax.

You must excuse this badly written letter as I am so weak and nervous that I can hardly sit up....

Do not come to the regiment until you hear from me again.

Your friend,

H. A. Macon

What made Henry Macon's news an even more tragic blow to James Ousby, was that shortly before receiving that distressing information, he had just been delivered of another letter—the last words his brother ever wrote. The missive consisted of one hurried page, and was headed "at Carlisle, Pennsylvania," less than four days before William was killed in action. The letter is happy and positive; he writes that food is plentiful, no fighting has yet occurred, and Ewell's Corps will "move on Harrisburg...where we expect the Yankees to make a stand." One of the last sentences reads: "Give my love to all your family and sisters and write and let me know how matters are going on at home. A letter directed to Richmond, Va. will reach me at some time or other."

No such letter, of course, would ever reach William Ousby. He was already dead, and his body was about to disappear as well. For incredible as it may seem, William's corpse, although interred very decently in Confederate held ground, soon seemed to vanish from the planet. This is particularly distressing, for the facts indicate that his grave was carefully attended to and precisely marked. Yet *no record* of that burial was ever recorded in the journals of Dr. John O'Neal, or in the final documented exhumations by Rufus Weaver, M.D.

So Captain William Ousby, who was accounted for in his last minutes, and in his hour of death, suddenly became lost to history. By some unexplained set of circumstances, he is now merely one of the more than 4000 unknown and forgotten Confederates whose identities were erased at Gettysburg.

HE SAID THAT HE WAS WILLING TO DIE

Corporal Leonidas Torrence,
Co. H, 23rd North Carolina Infantry
Iverson's Brigade, Rodes' Division, Hill's Corps

Combat was by no means a new ordeal for Colonel Daniel H. Christie of the 23rd North Carolina. But it must have been awful to witness, on July 1 at Oak Ridge, the destruction of his small, brave regiment. Numbering only 316, he saw it torn to pieces as he guided them toward the strong Federal line hidden and waiting their chance to fire. The assault was ill-planned from the beginning, and the Yankee bullets tore into the ranks of General Alfred Iverson's Brigade like a scythe through standing grain, mortally wounding Christie, and causing casualties in the 23rd to reach the astounding percentage of 89.2, one of the highest losses of any unit in the Battle of Gettysburg. In only minutes, Colonel Christie and 64 of his soldiers went down, killed outright, or doomed to face an inevitable death within days. One man whose injury would prove mortal was Corporal Leonidas Torrence, a Gaston County native who had already been hurt in battle at Sharpsburg, ten months earlier.

Unlike many of the men who died in Civil War battles, Corporal Torrence was fortunate that a comrade kept a record of his last hours for his family back home. This man was Corporal W. J. O'Daniel, who did not survive the war himself. In three finely detailed letters written to Leonidas' mother after Gettysburg, O'Daniel paints an accurate picture of his friend's wounds, and his final struggle. The first account was penned from Williamsport, Maryland, on July 9, 1863, during the retreat of Lee's army from Pennsylvania:

> Mrs [Sarah A.] Torrence
>
> I this eve take the present opertunity to drop you a few lines. Leonidas requested me to write when I left him.... Leonidas was alive when I left him but I think that he is not alive now. He was wounded in the head & thigh[.] His thigh [bone] was not broke but I could not tell what way the [shot] went. The ball in his head went in between his eye and ear. I think that it stopped some place near his brain. He came to his censis & told me that he was a going to die & gave me all his things except his testament and his pocket handkerchief. He told me to give his things to you....
>
> I wanted to stay & wait on Lon & [the other wounded] but the Doc would not let me stay[.] I waited on them from [the time] they were wounded untill Saturday. They were wounded on Wednesday. The Doc left S. G. Freeman to wait on them. Lon could not eat any thing. He drank water but he throwed it all up. He said that he was willing to die. I will have to close.... Write as soon as you receiv this letter.... I will write again the first opertunity[.]
>
> W. J. O'Daniel

How those few words must have broken the anguished heart of Sarah Torrence. "The ball...went in between his eye and ear." "I think that he is not alive now." Mere words, but how painful to her, more intense perhaps, than the physical pain that was endured by her own cherished son. The beloved face she once so tenderly kissed was now bloodied and disfigured, and the body she had given birth to, and caressed through his youth, now must occupy a commoner's grave in a foreign land.

On July 20, the army was again safely encamped in Virginia. It was there, at Bunker Hill, that Corporal O'Daniel sat down to correspond with Mrs. Torrence a second time:

I take my pen in hand to answer your letter that you wrote [to Leonidas] on the 6th of July. I am sorry that he was not her[e] to receive it. It hurts my feelings so that I hardly no what to write. I wrote you a letter as soon after the battle as I could.... Leonodous was shot between the Eye and ear and in the thigh. I think the ball that went in his head went near his brain. he did not know any thing for several hours. The ball in his thigh I think went into his body. This was the opinion of the Doctor.

L[eonidas] saw me when he came to his sencis.... He could not eat any thing. He drank a great deal of water but he throwed it all up. I got him some milk but it would not ly on his stomick. When I went to tell him goodby he told me that I would never se him again. He said he was a going to die. He also said he was willing to die. When he was shot he was lying in a hollow in a very mudy place. All that ware badly wounded and killed was shot in this same hollow. I was shot before the Regt [got] to this place[.] L and I went into battle side by side. We promised each other if one go[t] hurt to do all we could for him.

You doo not have any idea [how] I hated to leav Lon. I asked the Doctor to let me stay with him but he would not. Lon gave me his testament[,] pocket knife and pocket book to me and told me if he died to give them to you. He had $76 dollars in paper money, $1.33 in Silver.... I will take care of his things.... I will write to you as soon as our boys that was taken prisnors gets back. It may be that they will here from the wounded of our men[.]

The final letter was dated August 10, when O'Daniel was in camp with the 23rd Regiment near Orange Court House, Virginia. He had just received the first word from Sarah Torrence herself, and she apparently had some more questions about her son:

Your letter dated the 30th of July came to hand this eve. It found me well. Though verry lonesome. I have wrote you two letters since the Gettysburg fight. You wish to no if their was any Doctor left to wait on L. Their was one left to wait on the wounded of our Regt. The Doctor tole me that he could not do any thing for L's wound. The Doctor gave him medicen to make him rest. He did not appear to suffer a great deal. At times he would throw up and his bowels would get easy. He inclined to sleep the most of his time.... He was shot in the temple at the edge of the hair. It was a larg minney ball. The one in the thigh was the same kind.... I do not think that Leonodus could get well. he said himself that he could not get over it.

You wanted to know something about his bed.... He had a good tent that John Wilson gave me for L & [S. L.] McClure. They ware together in one tent. Leonodas had as good a *bead* [sic] as I could make out of blankets. he had severl blankets and a good oilcloth to ly on. He could not help himself but verry little. He was speechless for three or four hours. He maid sines for water when he wanted to drink.... I have wrote about all that I can remember as it has been some time since the fight. Evry thing is quiet here now. I fear it will not remain so long. Look over all errors. So nothing more at present, but remains as ever

W. J. O'Daniel

Reviewing the dispositions of all Confederates who died at or near Gettysburg, the "killed in action" of the 23rd North Carolina present us with a strange and perplexing puzzle: Where are their dead?

Fact number one: The 23rd lost 65 men killed outright and mortally wounded, a high percentage when you look over the totals for the rest of the 269 batteries, regiments, and battalions which made up the Army of Northern Virginia in the Gettysburg Campaign. Fact number two: Of those 65 deaths, we know the whereabouts of burial sites for only *two* of that regiment's dead. They were recorded by Doctors O'Neal and Weaver in the lists they drew up in 1863, 1864, 1866, and in 1871-73. The pair in question were interred in the cemetery of the U. S. General Hospital (Camp Letterman), east of Gettysburg, and a post-battle facility. None of the 23rd's men were found buried in any of Confederate field hospitals of Lee's army. One other known burial location was that of Colonel Christie, mentioned earlier. He died either on the retreat, or at Winchester, Virginia, and his body was laid in the cemetery at that place. So the same question remains: Where are the other dead?

In the late summer of 1871, 137 Southern remains were removed from the vicinity of Gettysburg by the Wake County (NC) Ladies' Memorial Society, and reinterred at Raleigh in October of that year. The two members of the 23rd North Carolina who died at Camp Letterman were among the 137. No other soldier from that regiment is on the roll. Among the hundreds of identified Confederate dead in the total of 3,110 taken to Richmond, Savannah, and Charleston, not one from the Twenty-third made these rosters. It is as if Corporal Torrence and 62 of his comrades just disappeared from the face of the earth.

That is not the reality, of course. It is much more mundane. Somehow, the few like Leonidas Torrence who made it back to field hospitals in the rear areas, were either buried without identification by strangers, or were placed in vulnerable spots where nature, or the plow, sealed their doom. So all were lost, both to their families, and to posterity, when their bones went undiscovered, or became mingled in the general shipments of unnamed and unknown remains sent to the South in the 1870s.

The other members of the 23rd who were killed instantly in battle were also interred without headboards to mark their passing. They were deposited into the bloody ground itself, in long shallow trenches, within the "muddy hollows" where they had fallen directly under the enemy's guns. These men met an equal misfortune, for lacking names and units, they too slipped into oblivion.

"Who they were, none know;
What they were, all know."

TO THOSE WHO LOVED HIM WELL

Private J. Rial Stewart,
Co. G, 23rd North Carolina Infantry
Iverson's Brigade, Rodes' Division, Ewell's Corps

The Civil War took a great toll on the fighting men of the Old North State. And the Battle of Gettysburg, although it was only one action among thousands fought during that conflict, was responsible for a large number of North Carolina's casualties. While the other Confederate states might have felt proud of the sacrifices they made battling for Southern independence, the Tarheel State went far and beyond any of them in the losses it sustained during that war.

The gradual chipping away of North Carolina's manpower at Gettysburg began early on July 1 along McPherson's Ridge, and by midday that state's troubles were escalating also on Oak Ridge, less than a mile northward. When General Robert Rodes' Division first arrived on Oak Hill, and, metaphorically, "uncoiled like a dangerous serpent," Rodes had at that moment an excellent opportunity to crush the Federal right flank in his front. But the general's tactics left much to be desired, and the quick destruction of one of his brigades led by General Alfred Iverson, was just the first blow of a hard day for the soldiers of his command.

Oscar Blacknall, the son of Major Charles C. Blacknall, of the 23rd North Carolina, later described that unit's demise. In his father's biography, Blacknall explained how Iverson's men advanced toward the Union force which was hidden from view, marching steadily across John Forney's farm fields, drawing ever closer to a stone wall on the crest of Oak Ridge. When the four regiments, the 5th, 12th, 20th, and 23rd North Carolina, reached a shallow depression, or hollow in the earth, which ran diagonally in front of the ridge, the trap was sprung. "[A] solid wall of blue,..." said Blacknall, "rose...and poured in a plunging, crushing fire. The range was point blank.... The effect upon the 5th, 20th and 23rd regiments was terrible, that one volley really striking down hundreds."

But the Tarheels, according to Oscar Blacknall, did not recoil. It was not simply because they stood their ground; more precisely, a retreat would have meant total annihilation. Instead, the trapped infantrymen took cover in the low ground, while the Yankees kept up a merciless fire upon their shattered ranks. It meant certain death to rise from a prone position, yet some of the wounded risked their lives and attempted to run to safety.

The colonel of the 23rd, Daniel Christie, tried to lead a charge to break the horrible stalemate, but he quickly fell mortally wounded. A lieutenant of Company I recalled that this "was the only battle of the war in which [I] ever saw blood run...and that too on the hot dry ground." Eventually, support was sent to assist the pinned-down brigade, but as General Stephen Ramseur's Confederate brigade closed in to help, the Yankees charged the depression and captured over 300 men, along with the colors of the 23rd. As the two sides collided and mingled, Ramseur's would-be rescuers shot indiscriminately into the milling soldiers, killing and wounding men wearing both blue and gray. One of those hit by "friendly" bullets, said Blacknall, was "Rial Stewart and perhaps other members of the 23rd who had been captured and were on their way to the federal rear."

The mortal wounding of J. R. Stewart by troops of his own country was very disheartening to his comrades. A sharpshooter in the regiment, Private John F. Coghill, gave more particulars of this incident in a letter composed on July 9 to "Pappy[,] Ma and Mit.":

> I regret to tell you that Rial Stewart was killed after he was takened a prisioner[.] the yankes took the best part of our Regt and Brigade and while they was carring them on to the rear wee had another line of battle marched up and shot a volly into the yankes and the prisioners and a ball hit Rial in the side[,] the ball went in one side and came out the other[.] he did lived some 4 or 5 hours after he was struck[.] he was in his right mind untill he died[.] some of our boys stayed with him untill he died[.] I never saw him no more after he went into the fight[.] Brother [Corporal K. W. Coghill] barried [buried] him[,] he was killed in the battle of gettysburg adams co. PA[.] I loved Rial as a Brother and I would do any thing that I could for him[,] he was a brave and knoble young man[,] but alas he has fallen in the cause of his beloved Country....

The following day, from Rockville, Virginia, Coghill again wrote to his family, informing them again about "the horrible place of Gettysburg," and how "toungs can not tell the horrors of that day." He also added more on Rial Stewart, saying he "seamed to be willing to die," and that "some one had taken his watch and his monney before he was found by eny of his company[.] but I have got his pocket book and took his rings witch I will take good care of untill I can send them home to those that loved him well...."

The story of J. R. "Rial" Stewart is a bad one, and another tragic piece of an already sad moment in American history. He was shot down by his own men just when his life might have been saved. But as his friend Coghill said, Stewart was a "brave and knoble young man." And evidently, Private Coghill was not the only one to notice Stewart's conduct in the battle. There is a sentence in J. R. Stewart's military service record which is rarely seen in the files of Union or Confederate soldiers who served during the Civil War in the years between 1861 and 1865. It read: "Posthumously awarded the Badge of Honor for gallantry at Gettysburg."

Private Stewart's final minutes of battle were framed in glory, but his death was tragic and unnecessary. And inasmuch as Stewart's death was a misfortune, his burial was what a soldier in those days both dreaded and expected. He, with many of his North Carolina companions, was interred where they had fallen, in long common graves within that blood-soaked hollow on John Forney's land. In 1897, Oscar Blacknall visited this area, the very place where his father had stood and fought, and was wounded and captured. Afterward, he wrote:

> Old Mr. Forney, who witnessed the battle, was then still alive. He was able to give me a very clear idea of all that part of it. He showed me the "Iverson pits" the trenches in which the brigades dead lay till years afterwards [when] they were removed to Richmond. The luxuriant growth of the bitter or smart weed marked their course and some of the pits still yawned.

This was also the place where "Rial" Stewart had died. In one of these trenches, his cold, lifeless body had laid, covered only lightly that year by the warmed earth of a Northern summer.

(gac)

Private Lewis Hill was one of Iverson's men captured, but he survived the battle.

32

IN THE HOUR OF HIS DEATH

Captain William P. Cromer,
Co. D, 13th South Carolina Infantry
Perrin's Brigade, Pender's Division, Hill's Corps

When the day ended on Wednesday, July 1, the men of Pender's Division were completely exhausted. They were hurting too, from the heavy losses inflicted on their ranks in the final sweep of battle from Herr's Ridge, then across McPherson's farm, and finally over Seminary Ridge and into Gettysburg itself. Later, as most of the men rested, details were organized and sent to the rear, and back over the contested ground to bury the dead and care for the wounded who had been left behind in the mad rush to overpower the Federal line.

One of the burial squads was led by Lieutenant Joel A. Walker of Company K, 45th Georgia, Thomas' Brigade. Once organized, Walker took his platoon out to McPherson's and began the unpleasant task of collecting the dead and preparing their graves. The first casualties they encountered were from Perrin's, (formally McGowan's) South Carolina Brigade, which were intermingled with some of the fallen Union defenders. Walker and his Georgians worked from corpse to corpse, eventually reaching the ground west of the Lutheran Seminary near John Herbst's woodlot, now called "Reynold's Woods." When close to the treeline, a curious sight caught the lieutenant's eye. In 1882, for publication in his hometown newspaper, Walker wrote down what he had seen:

> Our attention was then directed to a white hankerchief suspended over the face of a dead man. We approached to find that in the hour of his death some kind friend had fastened this hankerchief to a few straws, which kept the sun from burning his face, and his death had been so calmly he had not broken down the frail canopy. He was from Charleston, S. C., and bore the rank of a captain, but his name was nowhere to be found."

When this article was first discovered many years ago, the paragraph above spurred an effort to find the unknown captain. Initially, a survey was conducted of the nearly 3,900 named Confederates killed as a result of the battle. (The total number of dead is probably closer to 4,700, but presently only the lower figure is identified). This search resulted in only two South Carolina captains of Perrin's Brigade who could be accounted for as "killed in action" at Gettysburg. One of those officers was mortally wounded on July 2, which left 26-year-old Captain William Cromer as the likely candidate.

A history of McGowan's Brigade, written in 1866, revealed that only one captain died on the first day of the battle; he was "Capt. W. P. Compton" of the 13th Regiment. This name was obviously in error, for there was no such officer in the 13th. But by reading the letters of a surgeon of the regiment, it is verified that Captain Cromer was indeed lost on July 1. Additionally, a consultation was made of Dr. John W. C. O'Neal's burial lists, (1863-1866), to see if they could provide more evidence. However, his registers were silent in regard to this captain. That was to be expected, because Lieutenant Walker could not have marked the South Carolina officer's grave without a name.

Finally, and as a last resort, an examination of Dr. Rufus Weaver's "shipment rosters" was attempted. These papers include both named and unnamed Southern remains sent to Richmond in the early 1870s. Surprisingly, Cromer was among those transported; his bones had been shipped in a box marked "U," to Hollywood Cemetery. This discovery was baffling, because if Cromer lay in an unmarked grave, and went undiscovered by Dr. O'Neal, how could he appear on Weaver's inventory? Digging deeper into the three-year documentation notes assembled by Dr. Weaver, the mystery began to clear up. There, on one of his pages, written in next to the names in Box "U," was a clue: "6. S.W. cor. Seminary woods-." This information placed six graves in the correct location, and Weaver found them almost exactly where Walker's men interred the unknown South Carolina officer. On another sheet, however, Dr. Weaver finally gave the answer. Describing the contents of Boxes "T" and "U," (a total of 31 bodies), he wrote:

1 One T 16 A. P. Hill, McPherson's—to rear of Theological Seminary
1 One U 15   "   "   Oak Ridge—Among this number of Remains is Capt.
W. P. Cromer, 13th S. C.

There are several possible explanations for this strange remark, but only two seem logical. One, is that the person who placed the "hankerchief tent" over the captain, returned, found the grave already completed, and erected a headboard with Cromer's name and unit. But this supposition means that Dr. O'Neal must have missed the grave on several occasions in his rambles over the battleground in 1863, 1864, and 1866. Or two, Weaver or his exhumation crew found, mixed in among the bones of Captain Cromer, some identification overlooked in the hurried original burial by Lieutenant Walker's platoon. This often happened, as bodies and clothing were found still remarkably preserved even after ten years underground. The uniform pockets sometimes contained letters, diaries, testaments, various documents, and even money, watches, and jewelry. When Weaver added Cromer's name to his inventory, it was squeezed in between the two statements listed above, like an afterthought. In other words, almost as if the information had just been uncovered. This all tends to lead to the second conclusion above.

In any event, the whole story is fascinating. And it is hoped that by this investigation, another Confederate's "last moments" can now be presented to those interested in their particular chapter of our American heritage.

Lt. G. W. Wood, 60th Georgia, was hit in the lungs and liver and captured. His wounds were mortal and he died in the enemy's hands. (dwv)

The Casualties Of Day Two: July 2, 1863

SERVICE TOO SHORT

Private Joseph E. Love,
Co. F, 5th Texas Infantry
Robertson's Brigade, Hood's Division, Longstreet's Corps

Private Love did not lead a soldier's life for very long. On April 1, 1863, in Houston, Texas, Love, a 31-year-old Galveston resident, enlisted "for the war." He was immediately sent to his regiment in Virginia, a unit like many others which needed replacements badly. And just 92 days after volunteering, Joseph Love, with probably no combat experience to his credit, found himself taking part in the worst possible calamity of his life. On a July afternoon, the second day of the Battle of Gettysburg, he and 800 of his fellow Texans struggled to climb the rocky southwestern side of Little Round Top. In the deadly process, 247 of them were struck down by the plunging enemy fire. Love did not escape the carnage; he was hit in the face and right arm by enemy missiles, either bullet or shell, or perhaps both, say his records. So for him, one battle was over, and another, more terrible than the first, was just beginning. The fight had surely not been a picnic for anyone in Love's Company A, the "Bayou City Guards," for eighteen of his new companions were either killed or wounded on that day.

Many Federal accounts attest to the suffering of the Southern wounded who lay, after the fighting had ended, among the mossy gray boulders of the Round Tops. Eyewitnesses tell too, how men from the 44th New York, 83rd Pennsylvania, and other regiments crawled out to answer the anguished pleas of injured Texas and Alabama soldiers who were necessarily abandoned by their comrades. Among those rescued, after suffering what few can imagine, was Joseph Love.

On July 5, he and 75 other Confederates were taken to the U. S. Fifth Corps field hospital on the farm of Michael and Matilda Trostle, one mile south of the battlefield. The next day, Surgeon Edward Breneman, U.S.A., performed a "Circular Amputation of Rt Arm at the Upper 3rd." The procedure was needed due to a compound fracture of the humerus caused by the enemy projectile. After 20 days, Private Love, prisoner of war, was turned over to the provost marshal and sent by rail to Baltimore, where he became a patient in West's Buildings U. S. General Hospital. This facility consisted of six large warehouses at the foot of Jones Falls, with a capacity of 425 beds.

The medical log kept on Love confirms that he was received at the hospital with the above described arm injury, as well as, "A bullet wound destroying left Eye & opening cavity of the nose, accompanied by a Severe diarrhoea." Over the next three weeks Love's condition was complicated by the diarrhea, and by "great discharges" of fluids from the stump of his arm, even though the wound was said to be "almost entirely healed." Eventually the remaining bone, which was being drawn forward by the great pectoral muscle, produced so much pressure on the skin covering it that "sloughing" began, resulting in a gradual opening of the wound. On August 15, as Love's "power of reason" decreased, it was decided to re-amputate to correct the problem. Following this procedure on August 20, his condition was "much improved," with the wound healing, and the diarrhea subdued. However, on the 22nd, "the axillary artery was opened by a slight process of sloughing, & considerable blood was lost." Surgeon Edward Brooks quickly tied off the artery, but it was too late. Joseph Love lost the fight, and in an hour was dead of "exhaustion."

The following day he was buried in Loudon Park Cemetery, about three miles southwest of the hospital, on what is today known as "Confederate Hill." A latecomer to his country's call, Private Love nevertheless served faithfully. He had struggled valiantly in the forefront of the greatest battle of the war, and equally, in the toughest fight of his life.

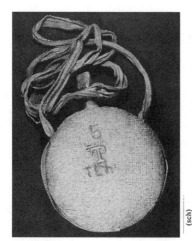

This canteen was Pvt. Love's closest companion as he lay dying on Little Round Top. It was later picked up as a souvenir of the battle. Joseph Love eventually died in Baltimore. There he received an excellent burial with a marble headstone.

HIS FACE TO THE FOE

Captain James H. Ellison,
Co. C, 15th Alabama Infantry
Law's Brigade, Hood's Division, Longstreet's Corps

It has sometimes been said that there is no good way to die. Considering how the majority of humans usually spend the final moments of life, that statement has great validity. Yet in every age there have been men who, if death must come, wanted to die as soldiers should in battle, fighting honorably, skillfully, and determinedly. And too, there were other men who fell in combat—their lives also important—but their wishes on that subject are unknown. When any of these soldiers went to their deaths, they were often remembered for their steadfastness of character and dedication to duty. J. Henry Ellison was one of these men.

Captain Ellison rose quickly through the ranks following his enlistment in 1861. Two years after that date, and nearing battle in the enemy's country, this former sergeant, and 26-year-old son of a distinguished Methodist minister, must have looked quite handsome toiling alongside his company as it moved steadily forward, toward the strong Federal position solidly anchored on the southern slope of Little Round Top. In fact, on that second day of July, he may have been the best dressed soldier in the ranks, for Captain Ellison was wearing a beautiful, brand new officer's jacket, trimmed with gold lace, presented to him barely a month earlier by his colonel, William C. Oates.

As the Confederates closed in on the rocky plateau held by the 20th Maine Infantry, and bullets from a withering fire tore into the Alabamians, Lieutenant Colonel Oates gave an order "to change direction to the left," so as to drive back this Union regiment. The noise of battle was too great, however, and Captain Ellison failed to understand the command. So he stepped up to Oates, leaned in, and cupped his hand behind his ear inquiring, "What is the order, Colonel?" Oates repeated it, and Ellison turned to his company and cried out: "Forward, my men, forward!" Writing almost 40 years later, Oates vividly described what happened next:

> I was looking at him when a ball passed through his head, killing him instantly. He fell upon his left shoulder, turned upon his back, raised his arms, clenched his fists, gave one shudder, his arms fell, and he was dead. His company gathered around him, notwithstanding they were exposed to the most destructive fire at that time. I ordered Lieutenant [Legrand L.] Guerry to place the men in line and order them forward.

The colonel ended his narrative with a personal expression of Captain Ellison's qualities and attributes. "I thought at the moment of his death that he was the handsomest and finest specimen of manhood that ever went down upon a field of carnage. [He] was one of the most esteemed officers in the regiment. All regretted his death."

Who could ask for a more perfect eulogy?

BROTHERS IN ARMS, BROTHERS IN DEATH

Privates G. A. & W. C. Jones,
Co. G, 5th Texas Infantry
Robertson's Brigade, Hood's Division, Longstreet's Corps

If anyone today still believes that Little Round Top should have been an easy capture by the Confederate forces sent against it on July 2, they would do well to pass over the recent flood of words concerning a certain Federal regiment there, concentrating instead on the "attackers" themselves, and read the "soldier narratives" of the Texans and Alabamians now available to the modern researcher. Frankly, to do so is to be overwhelmed by feelings of hopelessness regarding the tactical situation encountered there by the Southerners. On that fateful day, the participants clearly expressed the difficulties they faced on that bloody hill, when they met such an unexpectedly strong and determined Union presence there.

During the attack, for instance, one single regiment suffered an incredible 54 deaths. And it was in this unit, the 5th Texas, and on that hill, that a most grievous and unusual incident occurred. One of the Texans, Corporal John W. Stevens of Company K, observed the incident. He explained:

> As we start up the mountain we got a plunging volley from the enemy, who are posted behind the rocks on the crest. They are not more than 25 or 30 steps away and well protected by rocks, while we are exposed to their fire. Their first volley was most destructive to our line.... We are suffering terribly.... Only eleven men stand their ground [from Company K], but there we stand and fight for life. The balls are whizzing so thick around us that it looks like a man could hold out a hat and catch it full. There are two twin brothers belonging to Co. [G], of my regiment, that got separated from their own company. They came up to where I was standing and commenced firing. In a moment one of them is shot down by my side. The other brother caught hold of him as he fell and gently laid him down on the ground, and as he did he so he also received a death shot. This was a very affecting scene—those two boys were twin brothers, so much alike that you could hardly tell them apart. They were always

together—where you saw one you saw the other. They had passed safely through all the previous battles unhurt—now they died together.

One of the brothers was Private G. A. Jones. He had entered the service in 1861; W. C. Jones had enlisted almost a year later, as a recruit from Milam County. It is hard not to wonder, at the conclusion of this plain and unvarnished story, if G. A. Jones ever tried, when he wrote home, to dissuade his sibling from joining the army and "coming into harm's way?" Or, did he encourage W. C., through a sense of patriotism, to leave the relative safety of Texas, and to enter boldly into his country's fight for independence? Either way, these twins met an unhappy ending. By dying side by side, and in each other's loving arms, their end takes on an aura of wretchedness rarely matched in the annals of war.

> In peace they sleep—the brave unknown
> Beneath the verdant sod,
> Above them bends the azure zone—
> The starlit arch of God;
> They came not back who went to war,
> Those heroes brave and true;
> They fell beneath the Southern star
> Before the ranks in blue.

DO NOT MOURN MY LOSS

Sergeant John W. Moseley,
Co. G, 4th Alabama Infantry
Law's Brigade, Hood's Division, Longstreet's Corps

"In a materialistic age, when only the present seems to have any value, it may be pardonable...to exhume from the grave of memory an incident singular in its pathos and grand in heroism." With those words, written in 1898, and which ring true even today, 4th Alabama private William C. Ward began an account of the last hours of his friend and regimental comrade, John Moseley.

Sergeant Moseley commenced his career as a soldier in 1861, only twelve days after the fall of Fort Sumter. At 24, he was the unmarried son of a widow living in Marion, Alabama, where he had prospered as a book merchant. Leaving that comfortable life behind, he chose to follow the fortunes of his state, where, according to Private Ward, he "was always present for duty—was always in the march to meet the foe and never missed a battle."

Thursday, July 2, began early for the men of the 4th Alabama, as they awoke at two a.m. and joined the other four regiments of Law's Brigade on a march of more than 25 miles toward Gettysburg. The day was warm, and the mountain roads were rough and steep for these veterans of Hood's Division. On that long day, many good men fell by the wayside unable to sustain the searing pace. Already ill, Sergeant Moseley had a doubly hard time, but he struggled along nonetheless.

Just after four in the afternoon, with no rest, General Law's troops were finally thrown into the battle, fighting their way over some very tough terrain toward Little Round Top, their objective. Private Ward did not make it far before receiving a "sharp, electric pain in the lower part of the body." He fell "with a sinking sensation..." thinking, "This is the last of earth." But his head soon cleared, and while "Minie balls were falling through the leaves like hail in a thunderstorm," he saw a man "wearily and painfully lay down a few feet away." It was his messmate John Mosely. Upon asking why his sick friend was there, Moseley replied that he was exhausted and unwell, and could not keep up with the charging line of battle. Yet even in his poor condition, Moseley wanted to know if he could assist his wounded friend Ward, who was "lying in a pool...of blood." Ward told Moseley, "You can do nothing. Your place is with the company." Moseley immediately arose and went forward, and, "I never saw him again" explained Private Ward.

William Ward may have lost sight of John Moseley forever, but the possibility exists that an enemy officer in the 83rd Pennsylvania Infantry did see him again. In 1865 Captain Amos Judson wrote a history of his regiment, and in the book he recalled that a few of the Confederates who were shot close to the Union lines were taken in by the Pennsylvanians. "Among the number brought in," said Judson, "I remember a fine looking young rebel sergeant who had the bone in the right thigh broken by a minie ball." According to the captain, this sergeant and another Rebel were carried in together. They had suffered a horrible agony from their wounds, and had been found lying helpless covered in blood. Judson and another man made them as comfortable as was possible under the circumstances, until both Southerners could be sent to the nearest U. S. field hospital.

At one point, when the sergeant was being moved to a blanket on a bed of leaves, he screamed aloud as the intense pain hit him: "Oh men, for God's sake, do be careful. Oh my mother!" Judson noted that the appeal "was enough to rift the heart of a stone." The good captain spent a full page of his memoir on this incident, indicating that it must have made a strong impression.

While it cannot be known for sure that this "Rebel sergeant" was Moseley, there are enough similarities to believe it to be so. The list is impressive. First, the soldier was found close to the Federal positions, along with one other Confederate. Then, he was said to be about 21, nearly the right age, and evidently "descended of gentle blood," as a bookseller might be described. The wounded man also called out for his mother. This is not unusual, but Moseley was very close to his widowed mother. And finally, the 83rd Pennsylvania fought elements of the 4th and 47th Alabama regiments, units which lost only one sergeant who died in enemy hands. There is only one unanswered question. It is not known if the Confederate rescued by Judson eventually lived or died, as he does not say so directly. In any event, these facts are presented for us to ponder, while illuminating the often strange and fascinating connections found among Union and Confederate soldiers on Civil War battlefields.

After the battle, William Ward learned from the other Alabamian who was captured with Moseley, that the sergeant had fallen fatally injured "on top of the mountain just in front of the enemy's line." He also reported that both men had been taken to a Union field hospital where Moseley died on July 5. But before his death, John Moseley, thinking of his beloved mother then living in Buckingham County, Virginia, wrote a final letter:

Battle-Field, Gettysburg, July 4, '63.

Dear Mother

I am a prisoner of war and mortally wounded. I can live but a few hours at farthest. I was shot fifty yards from the enemy's line. They have been exceedingly kind to me. I have no doubt as to the final result of this battle, and I hope I live long enough to hear the shouts of victory before I die. I am very weak. Do not mourn my loss. I had hoped to be spared, but a righteous God has ordered it otherwise, and I feel prepared to trust my case in His hands. Farewell to you all! Pray God may receive my soul.

Your unfortunate son,

John

When the end came, according to Private Ward's informant, "his captors wrapped John in his blanket and gave him a soldier's grave."

No useless coffins inclosed their breast,
Nor in sheet nor in shroud we laid them,
But they lay like warriors taking their rest,
With their martial cloaks around them.

When Private Ward's tribute for John Moseley was written, thirty-five years had passed since the events he described had occurred. Ward was then much distressed at the lack of interest shown toward the Southern dead and to the veterans yet living whose sacrifices had cost them so much. "We are made to feel that it is a reproach to have followed the southern cross; to have fought and lost was to have been criminally wrong." John Moseley, he thought, did not deserve such treatment. He "had died on the field of battle, believing his cause was just," one of a long line of heroes unknown to fame on earth, who lie in graves unmarked. "Comrade! Brave comrade! Rest in peace! It does not matter that your country has forgotten you; you fought and died for the 'The Lost Cause.'"

42

Presently, at the start of the 21st century, the "reproach" for those who followed the Southern Cross seems to grow stronger each year. When and how this self-righteousness will end, is something fearful to contemplate.

A MAN OF MORE THAN ORDINARY ABILITY

 Lieutenant Colonel Benjamin F. Carter,
4th Texas Infantry
Robertson's Brigade, Hood's Division, Longstreet's Corps

An unusual notice appeared in a Gettysburg newspaper on August 4, 1863, just one month following the three-day battle. It was a singular curiosity because it announced the demise of an enemy soldier, a Confederate officer who had recently been an uninvited visitor in the community. The notice read:

> Death of a Rebel Colonel—Colonel Benj. F. Carter, of the 4th Texas regiment, died in the Academy Hospital at Chambersburg, Pa., on the 21st ult., from the effect of wounds received at the battle of Gettysburg. He was a native of Tennessee, and emigrated to Austin, Texas, in 1853, where he practiced law and rose to some distinction in his profession.

Lieutenant Colonel Carter must have been a man who impressed those he came in contact with. A soldier from his adopted state once wrote about Carter that no officer in the Texas Brigade "was more universally loved." Another described Carter as "a warm-hearted, humane man, well up in military matters, and a thorough infantry officer." The colonel's background indicates that he was a very public man, which may account for his popularity. Born in 1831 in Maury County, Tennessee, by the middle of the 1850s Carter had moved to Texas where he eventually graduated from Jackson College.

The period between the late 1850s and the Civil War were very busy for Benjamin Carter. During that interval he built up a law practice, married Louisa O. Rust, a woman from a prominent Texas family, served two years in the state legislature, and was elected mayor of Austin. Yet this busy, important, and bountiful life did not prevent Ben Carter from answering the urgent call of duty. In July 1861, the successful lawyer and politician left all behind and raised a company of infantry in Travis County, which became Company B, 4th Texas Regiment. A year later Captain Carter was promoted to major, then to lieutenant colonel on July 10, 1862.

In only a year, on July 2, 1863, it all came to an end. The law degree, the political experience, the family life, the military command, the sum total of his work, sacrifice, and experience, metaphorically evaporated into the dense warm air of a Pennsylvania summer's eve. There near Gettysburg, on the rough southwestern slope of Little Round Top, the 32-year-old lieutenant colonel met an adversary he could not appeal to or overcome. Just as Carter took command of the regiment from its injured leader, Colonel John Key, he was "severely wounded while crossing a stone wall near the base of the mountain." Shot in the face, and twice in the leg, the many careers of Benjamin Carter closed, and a new period began; a fight for survival and ultimately for life itself.

The extent of Ben Carter's injury, or how long he waited for help on that dismal day in 1863, has not been determined. The colonel was but another casualty, one of hundreds who went down fighting as his regiment and brigade were cut to pieces in that rocky, hostile, and inaccessible place. Carter was eventually rescued. His early hospitalization and care are unaccounted for, but he was probably carried to Hood's Division infirmary at the Plank family farm west of Little Round Top. At the field hospital, Carter's condition must have suggested that he could stand the long wagon trek back to Virginia, because he was one of the 6000 or so of Lee's men who found a berth in an ambulance on the retreat from Gettysburg.

Unfortunately for Colonel Carter, his ride back to Southern territory was short-lived. Most likely his physical condition prevented him from continuing the terribly distressing journey. Well into the night of July 4-5, the conveyance which carried the colonel pulled up to the farm house of Jeremiah W. George. Carter's ambulance was part of the Confederate army's almost 20 mile wagon train of wounded which had taken a detour on its route to Maryland. The train had left the Chambersburg Turnpike at Greenwood and then headed southeast on what was called the old "Pine Stump Road." This short cut took the cavalcade to New Guilford, then on to New Franklin, Marion, and Greencastle and points south. That route went past Mr. George's farm, and Colonel Carter was deposited there, for better or worse.

During Carter's tenure at Mr. George's, there is no record of the treatment, if any, he received. But a brief account is available which sheds light on some of the long hours he spent in the house. The person who left this description was Jacob C. Snyder, a neighbor who lived not far from the George place:

> I visited Colonel Carter frequently during his stay there. He was a man of more than ordinary ability. He had enjoyed the advantages of a fine education, and had great conversational powers.... In the discussion of "the principles of the secession heresy" as he termed it, which he often did with his companions, in my presence, I learned he was of the Alexander H. Stephens stamp. [Meaning he supported "states rights" and slavery, but opposed secession]. He was taken to Chambersburg in an ambulance, where he subsequently died.
>
> From Colonel Carter I obtained much information in relation to the battle of Gettysburg. He had received his wound in the first charge made by [General Evander] Law upon Little Round Top, from the "Devil's Den." They had

met a heavy repulse from that place, and when General Longstreet ordered General Law to charge the second time, the latter replied in these words: "General Longstreet, I regard a second charge a needless sacrifice of human life,—to lead men against one of nature's impregnable barriers so well manned and so bravely defended,—I disobey the order." "These," said Colonel Carter, "were the precise words used by General Law."

Information pertaining to the exact date of Carter's removal from Mr. George's farmhouse is not extant, but it is true that the colonel lost his life in the Academy General Hospital at Chambersburg on July 21. The hospital was housed in a large brick school building on the corner of East Queen and Third Streets, and had been so employed since the Battle of Antietam. At the time of his death, Lt. Col. Carter was under the care of a local doctor named Jeremiah Senseney. His burial took place in the Methodist Cemetery, and was carried out by his long time servant, Henry Johnson, who crossed over into Federal lines to care for Carter.

Does the colonel still lie in that Pennsylvania burial ground almost 1500 miles from his home? Since no record presently available points to an exhumation of his remains to Austin, that possibility exists, but is unlikely. It would seem more plausible that in the postwar years, his body was conveyed to his home, or to some other cemetery in the South. After all, Benjamin Carter was a bright and rising star of Texas. He was an adopted son, but was destined for greatness and continued recognition in service to his chosen land. This destiny was cut short by Yankee bullets, yet Texas surely owed him six feet of its good earth, perhaps to be paid for by the ones who stayed at home.

Where are they who went away,
Sped with smiles that changed to tears?
Lee yet leads the lines of gray —
Stonewall still rides down this way;
They are Fame's through all the years.

Col. Carter impressed all whom he met, even his enemies. (rkk)

I GRASPED HIS COLD HAND

Captain William A. Dunklin,
Co. G, 44th Alabama Infantry
Law's Brigade, Hood's Division, Longstreet's Corps

About mid-morning of July 4, members of the 118th Pennsylvania Infantry Regiment started with the rest of its brigade toward a picturesque section of the battlefield, known forever afterward as the "Devil's Den." When the battle ended just hours earlier, the 118th Pennsylvania had been stationed on the northern rim of Big Round Top, its third and final tactical position of the last three days. In moving toward Devil's Den, the regiment traversed a very rough section of the field over which the 44th and 48th Alabama regiments had fought through on July 2. This area contained, among other terrain features, a rocky gorge through which ran a stream called Plum Run.

"At the foot of the hill and in the gorge," wrote the historian of the 118th Pennsylvania in 1888, "there were thrilling, horrifying scenes of blood and carnage. The dead lay in all shapes and in every direction, some upon their faces, others on their backs, while others were twisted and knotted in painful contortions." He noticed, too, that many of these corpses were still locked in martial positions, some kneeling behind rocks and clutching muskets as if ready to fire, but now cold and stiff in death, with "sightless eyes" staring ahead at an unseen enemy.

The slaughter here probably came as elements of Law's Brigade faced not only Union cannon and rifles from the Den and beyond, but also the fire from Little Round Top above and to the east. From what the Pennsylvanians saw, there had been little protection "from such a deluge of bullets."

Another observant soldier of the 118th who was present there on July 4, was Captain Francis A. Donaldson. Writing home two weeks later, he described one spot in particular, where he believed a company of Confederates had halted and then gathered around its leader in preparation for "the desperate ascent of the hill." Every single one of these men had been killed, said Donaldson. "I counted thirty seven bodies, all dressed alike, in a course dark material with black felt hats...." What really caught his attention however, was one individual, a striking Southern officer:

> A little in front of these bodies, with his head resting on a stone, his body straightened out and hands folded across his breast, lay, as if asleep, one of the handsomest men I ever saw.... He appeared to be about 35 years of age, was dressed in gray cloth jacket and pants, neither showing much wear, and appeared to be at least 5 feet 10 inches in height, weighing, probably, about one hundred and seventy pounds. His face had been shaven upon the cheeks the day of his death, leaving

a splendid luxuriantly flowing chestnut beard upon his chin. The ball that had slain him had pierced his heart, passing thro' a letter in his breast pocket from which I learned his name to be Wm. A. Duncan, [sic] Capt. 44th Alabama Regt., and dated from Selma.... I cannot tell you how sad the fate of this fine looking soldier made me feel. Indeed I could picture to myself the anxiety of his family for intelligence from this terrible battlefield,...and I could fancy the long lapse of years without one word, without one sign from their dear one, and their heart sickness from hope deferred. At parting, I grasped his cold hand in mine and bid farewell to the noble form that lay stretched in death before me....

Captain Donaldson was correct in his assumption that Dunklin's loved ones would ponder his whereabouts, even if one day they got word of his death. Even today there is no known record of the burial of Dunklin's body or the recovery of his remains. He was, as it has so often been said, simply one dead man among the many who lay on that space of thin, stoney soil surrounded by a myriad of hugh, lichen-covered boulders. Donaldson's last regrets were for Dunklin's sad ending, as he stared into the captain's unseeing eyes, with their "fixed and glassy gaze." "I fear [internment] cannot be done," mused Donaldson, "as there are so many to bury that time will be wanting even to scatter a little earth over them all."

NOBLE, GENEROUS AND BRAVE

Corporal Samuel Thompson,
Dement's Maryland Battery
Latimer's Battalion, Johnson's Division, Ewell's Corps

Samuel Thompson must have had a sterling reputation prior to entering the Confederate army in 1861. As a comrade said of him then, "And who in Baltimore did not know the handsome fellow before the war? Noble, generous and brave, he was the life of every social gathering he attended. Sam Thompson was one of the happiest men on earth, and he was happiest when making others happy."

He *had* courage, sure enough. During the early part of the Gettysburg Campaign, the 1st Maryland Artillery Battery, commanded by Captain William F. Dement, engaged enemy troops with its four bronze 12-pounder Napoleons at the Battle of Winchester on June 14-15, 1863. After this action, Corporal Thompson, who had been on duty with the "first gun" of Lieutenant C. S. Contee's section, was mentioned in the report of Colonel J. Thompson Brown, Gen. Ewell's Chief of Artillery. Thompson was "to be praised," Brown said, for his "coolness and bravery on this occasion..." These sentiments were proper and worthy, but the true test for Sam Thompson and the 1st Maryland was yet to come.

Like Corporal Thompson, Private George W. Smith, an artilleryman of Jordan's Virginia Battery died at Gettysburg. (ts)

This ultimate trial came about seventeen days later on a small ridge just east of Gettysburg. And for the artillerymen of 19-year-old Major Joseph Latimer's battalion, July 2 would be as near to hell as any would ever get. Ordered at 4 p.m. into a position on Benner's Hill, a location which possessed no offensive or defensive tactical merits, the 16-gun battalion soon engaged Union cannon on Cemetery and Culp's Hills in preparation for Ewell's infantry assaults planned for later that evening. Coming immediately under an accurate and crushing Federal counter-battery fire, which was "like a severe storm raging in the elements," it was not long before Latimer fell mortally wounded, and his four batteries suffered a heavy loss of men, horses, and ordnance.

During the zenith of this brutal contest, Corporal John W. F. Hatton looked off to his left and saw something he would never forget:

> Corp Thompson was engaged during the firing in dealing out ammunition from the caisson. He was rather careless as to the closing the lid of the box immediately after extracting a round. He was warned by a comrade that he was running a great risk. His reply was "Oh nothing's going to hurt Sam! Sam's going to *Baltimore!*" A few seconds after he uttered these words with a light and joyful heart, a shell exploded in close proximity to his caisson, scattering sparks in every direction, some of which fell into the open limber box, causing it to explode—a sheet of flame, a terrific report, and all was over in a flash of lightening. As the smoke drifted away, the caisson was revealed in a wrecked condition—spindles of the axle twisted, wheels shattered and warped, ammunition boxes reduced to splinters and whirled out of sight, save a few black and burnt fragments scattered around, and the horses frantic, some wounded and tangled in the harness, [yet] no one reported himself injured. But a few yards away from the scene of destruction, was a form lying prone upon

the ground, clothes scorched, smoking and burning, head divested of cap and exposing a bald surface where used to be a full suit of hair, whiskers singed off to the skin, eye-brows and eye-lids denuded of their fringes, and the eyes set with a popped gaze, and facial expressions changed to a perfect disguise. Was he breathing? No! The body was warm and flaccid, but the spirit had flown from the care and scenes of strife to seek his "Baltimore." It was the body of Sam Thompson, the jovial soul.

A friend later added that Thompson's actions during the war had been "gallant," and remarked: "No soldier in the Confederacy left a better record, and none were more beloved by his comrades. Peace to his ashes!"

Whether or not Samuel's spirit "flew on to Baltimore," is a matter of each individual's own personal hope or belief. But, as far as his natural body is concerned, it, in fact *was* returned to his cherished city. Following the debacle on Benner's Hill, Thompson's corpse was loaded onto a battery vehicle and driven about a half mile northward to the farm of George Wolf, where it was buried alongside two other men of Latimer's battalion. Later in the year, when Dr. O'Neal was making his initial survey of Confederate graves around Gettysburg, he came to the three graves on the Wolf place. In his ledger book the doctor made a note of them. The top line read: "Saml Thomson Baltimore (Removed)." Right under that, and next to the other two soldiers, Amos Ridenour and Frederick Willey, O'Neal added: "These graves obliterated by Hospital."

This last entry was an explanation that when Camp Letterman U.S. General Hospital was established in mid-July, (it was located on Wolf's property, one mile east of Gettysburg), the construction of the facility destroyed the original burial sites. However, that being the case, O'Neal's first notation means someone came ahead of the hospital builders and took Thompson's remains home directly after the battle.

In the end too, it appears that Sam Thompson's last words *were* fulfilled, just not in the way he intended.

I KNEW HE WAS A GOOD SOLDIER

Private Rufus B. Franks,
Co. I, 4th Alabama Infantry
Law's Brigade, Hood's Division, Longstreet's Corps

A man will dutifully enlist in the army to defend his country. For months and years he suffers the discomforts, fatigues, and dangers of camp, the march, and battle. Finally the soldier is killed. Yet hopefully, his nation lives on, so the death is not wasted. His personal reward is nothing more than "a few feet of the vilest earth," and perhaps a word or two in a service record. Eventually, however, as his immediate family passes away, nothing remains for him but obscurity.

Almost every soldier faces a similar fate—a short chronicle of life and awareness—then nothing more. The exception is that in some cases a comrade never forgot a friend's brief existence and early death, and chose to crown him with some words of praise, or a tribute of sadness and loss. That is what these narratives represent, and that is what Private Franks was given.

Rufus Franks' military service is short and to the point. His record states that he was a student from Huntsville, Alabama, and entered into the Confederate army on April 26, 1861, just fourteen days after the start of the war. He is shown present with his company in every engagement in which the 4th Alabama participated prior to Gettysburg. Officially, that little information is all that exists. It will take the recollections of two fellow Alabamians to give R. B. Franks his place in history.

The first documented memory comes from Private William C. Ward of Company G. Ward discusses the advance of Law's Brigade from Seminary Ridge toward Little Round Top, at about four in the afternoon on July 2. The brigade had just completed an almost 30 mile march to get to the battlefield. General John B. Hood then ordered his division to attack the Federal left flank, and the men, including Law's Alabamians, stepped off toward the enemy. General Law's men were obviously in no condition to fight so soon, but duty overshadowed the physical limitations presented. Soon, according to Private Ward:

> The air was full of sounds.... In the din of battle we could hear the charges of canister passing over us with the noise of partridges in flight. Immediately to the right, Taylor Darwin,...suddenly stopped, quivered, and sank to the earth dead, a ball having passed through his brain. There was Rube Franks,...just returned from his home in Alabama, his new uniform bright with color, the envy of all his comrades, his gladsome face beaming as if his sweetheart's kiss had materialized on his lips, calling to his comrades; "Come on, boys; come on! The Fifth Texas will get there before the Fourth! Come on, boys; come on!" He shortly afterwards met the fatal shot.

The adjutant of the regiment, Lieutenant Robert Cole, was near Franks when he received the "fatal shot," but he did not realize it. His narrative completes the scene:

> During our third and last ineffectual effort to dislodge the enemy from his stronghold, there emerged from our scattered ranks a youth whom I well knew in our boyhood days, Rufus Franks. He walked erectly and rapidly to the rear, still grasping his rifle, with no apparent evidence whatever of being the least wounded. A man hard hit invariably will drop his gun. As he brushed past me he remarked in a trembling voice, his face deathly pale, "Adjutant, a handful

of men cannot drive those Yankees from that place. Can't you get Major [Thomas] Coleman to call the boys off before all are killed?" I knew he was a good soldier, yet his actions forced me to imagine, "There goes a soldier whose heart is gone." I called in a rather pleading tone to him to come back. Without looking or stopping, and still with his gun at a trail, he replied, "I am wounded." Thinking he was only slightly wounded, I dismissed the incident, and in the confusion of battle would henceforth have been forgotten, had I not learned, as we lay in our rude breastworks of rock the next morning that he was shot in the bowels and died soon after he was taken to the hospital. Lieutenant Henry Roper,... while we were climbing up the mountain side, was shot through the lungs and incapacitated for duty ever afterwards. He informed me that he and Franks were taken from the base of Little Round Top in an ambulance to the field hospital. Although Franks knew he was mortally wounded, it was perfectly pathetic to hear him repeatedly apologizing to Roper between violent spasms of vomiting in the ambulance for his unavoidable demeanor.

Because Private Franks made it alive to the field hospital of Hood's Division on the farm of John Plank, he received a decent burial upon his death, with a headboard to mark the grave. And due to these fortuitous circumstances, Rufus Frank's remains were still identified eight years later. Therefore, when Dr. Weaver recovered and transported thousands of Confederates to Richmond between 1871-73, R. B. Franks made the trip in a wooden shipment container marked "2-H." He never got home to Alabama, but the box his remains occupied held the bones of four Confederate soldiers of the 4th Alabama, two from Arkansas, one from North Carolina, 10 from Texas, and 47 from Georgia.

Good company to be in.

IT WAS A PAINFUL SIGHT

Lieutenant Jesse H. Person,
Co. E, 1st North Carolina Cavalry
Hampton's Brigade, Stuart's Cavalry Division

In the waning hours of the late afternoon of July 2, the most intense, desperate, and important fighting of the Battle of Gettysburg occurred south of the town, on the left flank of the Union army's hooked-shaped defensive line. There, General Hood's Confederates struggled to overcome arduous terrain and stiff enemy resistance south and southwest of Little Round Top, through Devil's Den, and across Rose's woods and nearby wheatfield. What is not commonly known is that at the height of that fearsome combat, at that exact time, a separate and distinct military action was in progress almost six miles northeastward, near the village of Hunterstown. It was there that an exhausted cavalry brigade under General Wade Hampton, of General J. E. B. Stuart's Division, attempted to prevent a division of Federal horsemen led by General Judson Kilpatrick from flanking the left of Lee's army. The skirmish at Hunterstown lasted only a couple of hours, but it will forever be remembered as a classic cavalry fight, quick, fierce, and boldly contested.

One remarkable feature of that little battle was the relatively high percentage of Southern officers who were either killed or wounded. In one of Hampton's regiments alone, that of Cobb's Georgia Legion, six subaltern's became casualties, quite a large number for such a small fight. But this story is not about one of these Georgians—it concerns the death of a 21-year-old lieutenant named Jesse Person in one of General Hampton's other units, the 1st North Carolina Cavalry. Person's last moments of life, and his body's subsequent disposition, was chronicled in a descriptive letter written by an officer in Company E, Lieutenant Cadwalader J. Iredell. It was mailed to former lieutenant Robert J. Shaw, a friend of the deceased who had resigned from the army in the fall of 1862:

> Near Hagerstown, Md.
> July 7, 1863
>
> Dear Shaw,
>
> I write to you now to ask you to inform his family of the death of Lieut. Person. I know it will pain you to do so as it pains me to ask such a request, but I know of no one else there that could do so. It was a painful sight to us to see him breathe his last. The Brigade made a charge, our regiment being in

Lt. Person was buried somewhere in this Hunterstown cemetery. (sch)

front, with our squadron in front of the regiment. In the charge he fell pierced through the head with a ball. I did not see him fall, but a moment afterwards found him fallen from his horse, and dying, with Jasper Upchurch near him crying like a child. I immediately stopped some men and had him taken from the field. He expired just after reaching the hospital. He never spoke after he was shot. We have lost in him a gallant brave officer. This charge was made last Friday [sic] evening near Hunterstown Pennsylvania, he was buried the next morning in the Presbyterian grave yard at that place. Every attention was paid the body that could be under the circumstances. We fell back the morning he was buried, the grave was marked....

The few soldiers interred in established Gettysburg/Adams County cemeteries usually fared well, as the survival rate of their names and gravesites was higher than normal in the years following the battle and the war itself. But in the case of Lieutenant Person, that may not be so, as there is nothing so far yet found to provide the present location of his final resting place. It is curious that his name was not listed in Dr. O'Neal's several burial registers. Similarly, Person is absent from Dr. Weaver's shipments of Confederate remains to Richmond or Raleigh.

Therefore, unless family members or friends traveled to the North to secure his body and return it to Franklin County in North Carolina, Jesse Person may still occupy an unmarked and long lost grave at Hunterstown, Pennsylvania, hundreds of miles from home.

HE WAS GAME TO THE LAST

Unknown Negro,
Longstreet's Corps

In studying the fascinating world of Civil War literature, the facts are undisputed that thousands of Americans of African descent took an active and important role in the military affairs of both Northern and Southern armies between the years 1861-1865. On the Federal side, over 180,000 blacks enlisted to fight for the United States. Thousands more assisted the Union war effort in civilian capacities, as cooks, laborers, teamsters, and similar non-combat roles. In the Confederate States it was no different, except slaves and even freedmen could not legally be enlisted into the Southern army.

However, that technicality may not have prevented these "men of color" from actually fighting. More and more evidence has surfaced over the years indicating that some blacks actively participated in military actions as "members" of Confederate units. That premise may be confusing. But it would be naive to believe that out of four million Negroes in the South in 1860, not one ever acted as a "soldier" for the Southern cause. Even historian Robert K. Krick included "James Godman, Negro," in his 1981, "Gettysburg Death Roster." Godman, who died in a U. S. hospital after the battle, was moved with thousands of Confederate remains to Richmond's Hollywood Cemetery in 1872. And more to the point, a New York *Herald* reporter felt compelled to write the following in a news column after returning from the battlefield: "Washington, July 10, 1863. Among the rebel prisoners who were marched through Gettysburg there were observed seven negroes in uniform and fully accoutred as soldiers."

In that light, here is a story recognizing one man, who, for whatever reasons, *was present* in the battle on the Southern side. He was wounded grievously, and died bravely among veterans of Lee's army.

This most unusual account comes from Sergeant Edward Bragdon of the 10th Maine Battalion. After the battle, he led a detail of 38 men who were assigned to the U.S. Twelfth Corps field hospital on the Anna and George Bushman farm one mile east of Little Round Top. From July 4-14 Bragdon's assemblage worked there in various ways assisting the medical staff.

On or about July 15, the sergeant took leave of his duties and went for a walk westward out toward the Round Tops. Along the way he happened upon a small barn that was at one time in use as a Union aid station during the combat of July 2. It had been abandoned by the medical corps, but the interior still held 15 men. Two were dead, and the remainder were seriously injured, most missing an arm or leg. All were desperately in need of water after days of lying helpless and deserted.

This barn possibly sat on the farm of John Group, as records show several Southerners buried nearby, including Private S. G. Solley of the 47th Alabama. Sergeant Bragdon's "find" was probably a group of Gen. Evander Law's infantrymen, because, according to their own explanation, all were wounded in the attack on Little Round Top. When captured, they had been carried back to the Union rear to undergo surgical operations or other medical treatment. After the surgeons vacated, a local woman and a hurt soldier provided aid for a few days. When those resources failed, they were left alone and evidently overlooked when the wounded were being collected and consolidated.

As they cried out for water, the sergeant found a canteen and hurried to a nearby spring. For his actions, Bragdon said, "How those poor fellows did bless me!" In all that suffering, however, one scene impressed him above the rest. Here, in his own direct and few words, is Sergeant Bragdon's strange and distressing discovery:

> In another part, [of the barn], in the calf pen, was a darkey whose leg was gone nearly to the body. He had plainly suffered a great deal and his skin was changed to 'old gold' color, but he was game to the last and was full of gratitude to me.

Naturally, with stories like these, there are no good endings. All are tales of soldiers killed in battle, or who died suffering from serious wounds. Yet in this particular account, the *presence* of a black man enduring such a crushing injury in such a miserable and out-of-the-way environment cannot be explained. So there will always be questions. Was he among strangers or friends? How did he come to suffer such a horribly serious wound? And finally, was he fighting as a combatant when it happened, or was he a manservant or innocent bystander who just happened to be in the wrong place at the wrong time?

There are no answers here, only more questions.

> And for the country's honor fought
> The black man once a slave
> Encouched within the history's folds
> The statement, "he was brave!"

HE DIED IN MY ARMS

Private Samuel H. Watson,
Co. E, 5th Texas Infantry
Robertson's Brigade, Hood's Division, Longstreet's Corps

For a Confederate mortally wounded at Gettysburg, Private Watson was as about as far away from his family as a man in Lee's army could get. But for all that, his mother in Washington, Texas, got two things that very few in the same situation might expect. Harriet Watson received a detailed summary of her son's final days, and she found out that he was cared for in the best possible way before his death. Regarding a wartime casualty in enemy hands, these are comforts above and beyond what most could hope for.

General Robertson's Brigade faced combat at Gettysburg as difficult as any unit experienced in the battle. Some of his regiments hit stiff Union resistance at Devil's Den, while the balance assaulted the "Gibraltar" that was Little Round Top. The death toll of the brigade was remarkable, a total of 152, with Samuel Watson among the number.

When Watson was shot in the right arm while engaging Yankee troops on Little Round Top, he could not be rescued by his comrades. Captured by the Federals, Private Watson probably ended up in one of their Fifth Corps field hospitals where his arm was amputated on July 15. Later, he was removed to the general hospital at Camp Letterman a mile east of Gettysburg. There, the 21-year-old Watson was placed into a ward on the Third Division where he came under the care of nurse Euphemia M. Goldsborough, a Marylander and Southern sympathizer. Miss Goldsborough, or Effie as she was called, had begun her duties there on July 21, and must have taken an immediate liking to this young Texan. Her first record of him was noted in a hospital "diary" sometime in early August, when she wrote: "Samuel Watson, 5th Texas Regt. Lost his right arm. One of the most attractive boys I ever saw. Very ill. But little hope of his recovery but hope for the best." On September 9 she mentioned that he was "much better today. Strong hope of his recovery." But within a few days everything had changed:

> Died Sept. 13th, Sundown Sunday afternoon, 1863. Buried in grave no. 3 commencing at the right. 8th Section. My poor lost darling. Would to God I could have died to save you, but all is over, worldly sufferings are ended. If tears or love could have availed, I [would] not [have] been left to weep by his graveside.

Within a few days of Watson's death an exhausted Effie Goldsborough returned to Baltimore; she had spent nine weeks of diligent labor among the wounded of Gettysburg. But it would be almost ten years before the young Texan's remains were carried to Richmond for a final burial in Hollywood Cemetery. However, for Effie, there was one last duty to perform. She had to write the bad news to his mother. This poignant letter must have been both a curse and a comfort to the poor woman who would never see her son again. With its melancholy content, it remains today one of the most beautiful expressions of its kind ever sent in remembrance of a dead soldier from the terrible battlefield of Gettysburg. Mrs. Watson surely treasured it until the end of her life.

Mrs. Harriet Watson,

I suppose you have already received intelligence of your son, Sam H. Watson being wounded at the battle of Gettysburg. His right arm was amputated and for a time he seemed to be getting on nicely, but unfortunately for himself, and those who loved him, an abscess formed under his arm, which, with sorrow be it said, terminated his young life. It was my privilege to nurse him six weeks, during which time I looked to his comfort as I would my own *only brother* and learned to love him *just the same.* He died in my arms, Sunday evening, Sept. 13, *just at sunset* his precious brown eyes fixed in mine, without a struggle, and his last fleeting breath I caught upon my lips. He spoke of both you and his sister during the day and asked his cousin, Thomas Sneed of Texas, to return to you two plain gold rings that each had given him. Also a likeness of himself taken about five months back & to say "he had come for a soldier, *done his duty* and died for his country." I know every word I am writing will carry *grief to your heart*, and yet, judging you by myself, I feel that you would like to know all. I had him buried with my own, the Episcopal Church service, & marked his grave. Mrs. Watson, you *must not* feel that your son died in an enemy's country with *none* to *love* or care for him. His whole Brigade loved him as did all who came in contact with him, *even those* who were opposed to the glorious cause for which so many brave and noble have already been sacrificed, and many were the bitter tears shed over his untimely grave. If this should ever reach you, may I ask that you will answer it. I hope that we may meet after this unhappy war is ended and that I may be able to give you back your *darling son's* dying kiss. Hoping I may hear from you and with a heart full of sympathy and sorrow for your loss, with profound respect I remain,

Your friend
E. M. Goldsborough

WHAT MESSAGE DO YOU WANT TO SEND

Private Jackson B. Giles,
Co. C, 9th Georgia Infantry
Anderson's Brigade, Hood's Division, Longstreet's Corps

About an hour prior to General Hood's attack on the Union Third Corps, (the extreme left of the Army of the Potomac on July 2), Anderson's Brigade was moved into a wooded area in rear of Seminary Ridge. This position was behind a line of batteries which were engaged with enemy cannon in and near a peach orchard along the Emmitsburg Road. One of the batteries nearest to the Georgia regiments of Anderson's Brigade was the Troup Artillery of Athens, Georgia. This tactical deployment drew fire from the Federal guns, which in turn, endangered the Confederate infantrymen nearby. It was here, between about three and four in the afternoon, that the 9th Georgia sustained its first casualty in the Battle of Gettysburg.

That man was Private Jackson Giles, a "genial and bright" young fellow who had been detailed as a mounted courier for General George Anderson. Giles was very popular with his comrades in the 9th, mainly for his cheerful attitude, his willingness to perform the duties of a soldier, and for the positive way he participated in the daily interchanges of army life.

Captain George Hillyer, one of the regiment's company commanders, had the misfortune to see Giles when he was struck by an artillery projectile. Hillyer was particularly affected by the incident, for he had attended school with Giles in Monroe, Georgia. Years later, the captain explained his feelings in more detail:

> [I]t is to me still more interesting to speak of those whom I knew in childhood and boyhood and in the peaceful walks of life, in the town and neighborhood where we lived and grew up together; and when, indulging in our boyish sports, it was never realized or even dreamed that we were to be actors together in tragedies like these.

The killing of Jackson Giles happened during the exchange of cannon fire between the Troup Artillery and the Yankee gunners near Joseph Sherfy's orchard. As Giles passed around the left flank of the Ninth; he then dismounted, probably with the intention of visiting with friends who were taking cover from the deadly missiles that were tearing through and splintering the trees above their prostrated ranks. Captain Hillyer's account continues:

> Just then [a] shell...tore away his left leg above the knee and dashed him ten or fifteen feet down the hill. I got up and ran to him and instantly saw, by the pallor of his face and the physical shock he had suffered, being a rather

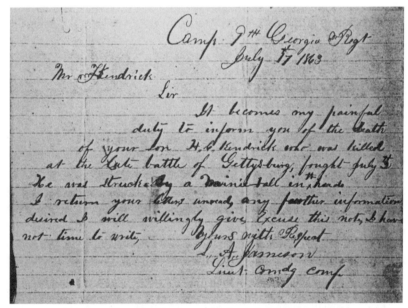

Few letters announcing the death of a soldier have survived.
But they were so important to the families that received them. (gnmp)

delicate youth anyway, that he would not survive the injury. So I placed him in as easy a position as possible and told him that as soon as the litter corps came to tell them I said carry him back to a hospital, and added, "Jack, you know we are going to make a charge in a few minutes, but if I ever get back to see your father and mother what message do you want to send them?" A distinct animation came into his face as he looked straight at me and said, "Tell them I died for my country."

In the words of the captain, "young Giles died at the hospital that same night." Regrettably, the exact location of this hospital is unknown. Anderson's men were, in the main, being sent to the field hospital of Hood's Division at the John Edward Plank farm along Willoughby's Run and south of the Fairfield Road. But a perusal of the burial records do not list Jackson Giles among the burials there. Nor was he included in the shipments of remains to Richmond or Savannah in the 1870s.

Remembered in life, but lost in death, Private Giles' last brave words were eventually brought home by the boyhood friend who survived the war. There his dying statement was surely cherished by a broken-hearted family. And on many a night, as they gathered for the evening meal, or sat around a crackling fire discussing the events of their lives, those manly sentiments were undoubtedly echoed as a consolation to the hurts of all.

IN A BEAUTIFUL GROVE

Major Donald M. McLeod,
8th South Carolina Infantry
Kershaw's Brigade, McLaw's Division, Longstreet's Corps

It would have seemed most unlikely to a passing traveler, especially for anyone not expecting it, to come suddenly upon the grave of a Confederate officer all alone in the quiet countryside of rural Pennsylvania. But had the person stopped for water at the farm of Mr. Jeremiah W. George, on the road from Gettysburg to New Franklin, between July 4, 1863, and April 20, 1866, the grave would have been impossible to miss. For there, "buried close by the well in a beautiful grove,... marked by a headboard bearing his initials," was the resting place of Major McLeod, formerly of Hunt's Bluff, on the Pee Dee River in eastern South Carolina.

A descendent of Scots ancestors who came to America in 1775, McLeod was 39 and married in 1861. In 1853 he had earned a degree from South Carolina College which enabled him to teach school; this he did until he began farming sometime before the war. When secession split the country, Donald McLeod was the first in the Marlboro District to raise troops for the state. The six foot, four inch tall officer was described as, "of commanding presence,... erect, active, and alert, beloved by his company, [who], when the test came proved himself worthy of their love and confidence." Within a very short time, due to the reorganization of the 8th, McLeod left Company K to accept the post of regimental major, a rank he held at Gettysburg. More than half a dozen battles had already tested McLeod, and on those past fields he had "exhibited undaunted courage," and was "faithful to every trust."

On July 2, Kershaw's Brigade took a prominent role in General John Hood's collision with the Union left flank, which stretched in a jagged line from Little Round Top to the Emmitsburg Road at Sherfy's peach orchard. More than an hour after the assaults began, Kershaw's and then Barksdale's regiments charged toward the Peach Orchard, with Major McLeod and the 8th South Carolina on the left of his brigade. Within minutes, even as this sudden movement dislodged the Federals, the major and over 100 of the 8th were hit by gunfire. Although several later writers reported McLeod as killed outright, he was in fact alive but severely wounded. His brigade commander remembered that McLeod acted that day as "a gallant and estimable officer."

It is unclear where Major McLeod was taken for medical treatment, but it was probably to Francis Bream's "Black Horse Tavern" on the Fairfield Road. Since many of the ambulances were collected along this thoroughfare at the start of Lee's retreat, it seems certain that the major was put aboard one of these conveyances to be carried to Virginia. It was not Donald McLeod's fortune, however, to make it very far. Once through Fairfield, the train of wounded crossed South Mountain and then turned off toward Greencastle. When not too distant from New Franklin, a halt was made at the aforementioned Mr. George's. There, several Confederates who had died along the torturous route were buried. Among those deceased was Major McLeod, who was interred by his servant at J. W. George's.

According to Jacob B. Snyder, a neighboring farmer, the death of the major caused his wife, Margaret C. Alford McLeod, to partially lose her mind. Therefore, in the spring of 1866, to ease her burden, Mrs. McLeod's brother and a friend, with McLeod's former servant as a guide, made the trip from South Carolina to recover the body. Mr. Snyder, telling the story in 1886, said:

> [They] followed up the way of the disastrous retreat until they came to Mr. George's, where the guide at once recognized the place and took them to the grave. The remains were taken up, carried to a place near my spring, and there prepared and enclosed in a box and taken along.

> I'se gwine back to Dixie,
> For I hear the children calling,
> I see the sad tears falling,
> My heart's turned back to Dixie,
> And I must go.

IN GREAT DISTRESS

Captain C. M. Ballard,
Co. C, 8th Georgia Infantry
Anderson's Brigade, Hood's Division, Longstreet's Corps

On the night of June 30, one of the spearhead units of General Robert E. Lee's Army of Northern Virginia was the North Carolina brigade of General J. Johnston Pettigrew. Just that day, this brigade had left Cashtown, a place that John R. Lane, the lieutenant colonel of the 26th North Carolina called, "the most beautiful position for Gen. Lee's army to make a stand that we had ever seen." Unfortunately for the Confederate army, and as subsequent events would bear out, Pettigrew's Brigade went into bivouac that night not at Cashtown, but about three miles west of Gettysburg on the Chambersburg Turnpike. Lane did not know it at the time, but he would visit the area of this bivouac again very soon, as a casualty instead of an invading warrior.

While in camp that evening, he made some mental notes of the site. The span of 27 years did not dim his keen memory, for in 1890 the former Colonel Lane was able to describe the site perfectly: "[Our halt was] just this side of a little creek crossed by a stone bridge where we filed to the right and encamped for the night in a beautiful grove, just in rear of a little field." The following morning, July 1, at daybreak, Lane remembered that, "We crossed the stone bridge, and just as we reached the summit of the hill beyond, opposite the brick house, afterwards one of [General A.P.] Hill's hospitals, the enemy opened fire on us...."

The rest is history, as they say, for Pettigrew's four regiments went on that day into an engagement which was to become one of the greatest battles ever fought in North America. The losses of the brigade were perfectly astounding, 1450 out of 2581 present. Lane's own regiment, the 26th North Carolina, had the single highest regimental casualty figure in the battle, 687, including its colonel, Henry Burgwyn. Lane, as was mentioned, did not escape this slaughter. After Burgwyn went down, Lane, cheered by the success they were having in breaking the Union line, ran up ahead of the 26th. "I turned to encourage my men when I was struck in the back of my neck by a ball which passed through into my mouth, knocking out all my teeth, upper and lower, beyond the center."

By evening Colonel Lane had been removed to the rear. Though he does not say where, it was probably to the "brick house" near the little stream, which was a tributary of Marsh Creek, the same building he had noticed that morning. Two sources indicate that it had to be a "house," because, for one, Lane himself states that during the great bombardment preceding the "Pickett-

Pettigrew Charge" on July 3, the "concussion [from the guns] broke out the window panes in the hospital...at a distance of three miles from the battle field."

There seems to have been no one single and definitive medical facility for Hill's Corps, especially since his men were engaged both July 1 and 3 on widely different parts of the field. The injured were therefore somewhat scattered, but mainly could be found on farms along the Chambersburg Pike between two and four miles west of Gettysburg. One of those was the newly built brick house of Charles B. Polley, a farmer who lived on the north side of the pike just east of the creek crossed by Pettigrew's men earlier that day.

During the time that Lt. Col. Lane languished in the hospital, a strange event occurred, which directly relates to the person characterized in the present story—26-year-old Captain C. M. Ballard of Macon, Georgia. One historian of the 26th North Carolina who had known Lane, gave the account as the colonel related it:

> When taken from the field, Colonel Lane was carried to the field hospital, a brick house. A wounded Georgia officer, who was lying near the door of the room in which Colonel Lane was, had been delirious all the morning. He finally became quiet about 1 p.m. [on July 3] and after a silence of some minutes, Colonel Lane heard him say in a perfectly rational tone of voice: "There now there now. Vicksburg has fallen, General Lee is retreating and the South is whipped." He ceased speaking and in a few moments an attendant passed by and said he was dead. General Lee did not retreat from Gettysburg until the evening of the 4th of July, and Vicksburg was not surrendered until the 4th of July."

Curiously, looking deeper into this event, one pertinent fact stands out that could be the element needed to identify the "unknown Georgia captain" who made the eerie prophesy. Only one field hospital in the place Lane described has been found which contained wounded from both Georgia and North Carolina. It was the farm of Charles Polley on the Chambersburg Pike, and the burials around his house were from those states. One of the graves listed by Dr. John O'Neal held the remains of "Capt C M Ballard 8 Geo. Regt." He had been interred in the "lower part of [the] orchard under two apple trees," and next to Lt. Col. William T. Harris, 2nd Georgia Infantry. Both officers were wounded on the afternoon of July 2, fighting with Hood's Division between Rose's wheatfield and Sherfy's peach orchard. How they managed to end up on the Chambersburg road is a mystery, because the majority of Hood's casualties were clustered further south along and below the Fairfield Road.

In any event, a definite eyewitness to Captain Ballard's last moments was a Georgia quartermaster named W. Edgeworth Bird. In a letter dated July 7, Bird told his wife Sallie that Ballard's brother Walter was present too at the time of death. Then Quartermaster Bird went on to explain that the dying captain was "in great distress. "I assisted as best I could," said he. "Held [his] legs while they were taken off." Bird also helped with the burial of Col. Harris.

Dr. O'Neal's register shows that both Georgians were eventually removed to the South. The records do not indicate Colonel Harris' final interment site, but Captain Ballard's remains were exhumed in 1871, and reinterred August 21 of that year in Laurel Grove Cemetery, Savannah, GA, Lot # 854, Grave # 13.

And yes, of course, his "prophesy" did come true.

I COVERED HIS FACE

Lieutenant Colonel Francis Kearse,
50th Georgia Infantry
Semmes' Brigade, McLaw's Division, Longstreet's Corps

"[I]mmediately after the fierce strife had ceased," wrote John Howard Wert, "[I] wandered over these fields...and the vivid impression of the horrible sights there beheld can never be effaced from the memory." This 22-year-old local teacher was speaking of the area around the farmstead owned by Dorothy and George Rose, west of Little Round Top, but which was being worked during the battle by George's brother, John Rose. He observed that the dead were everywhere, with "Festering corpses at every step; some still unburied; some, hastily and rudely buried...the appearance presented was almost as repulsive as where no attempt at burial had been made." Continuing, Wert described the graves near the stone structure itself:

> In the garden of the Rose house in full view,...nearly one hundred rebels were buried. All around the barn, even within the house yards, within a few feet of the doors, were in numbers, the scantily buried followers of the Confederate cause. Two hundred and seventy-five were buried behind the barn; a rebel colonel was buried within a yard of the kitchen door.

In all of his writings on the aftermath of the Battle of Gettysburg, J. Howard Wert was basically accurate and usually truthful. But in the last sentence above, in order to "thrill" the reader, which he often tried to do, Wert continued to perpetuate a myth. The story of those bodies on the Rose farm was not totally factual, and had probably begun to be spread around in May 1866. At that time Wert made the claim that a Gettysburg newspaper editor had written an advertisement for the sale of Rose's farm. The editor was reported to have said, among other things, that the land contained "Fifteen hundred rebels...buried on this very spot...one Confederate Colonel being buried within a yard of the kitchen door."

The "rebel colonel" was, in fact, Lt. Col. Francis Kearse, who began his military career as a private in the 50th Georgia. But Kearse had not been interred at the doorstep of Rose's house. Various people actually saw and commented on the real location of the grave of Francis Kearse.

One of the first to record Kearse's original gravesite was a civilian from Baltimore named Ambrose M. Emory. On a visit to Gettysburg in August 1863, Emory made a notation in his diary on the 19th, that in "passing over the field in front of the Round Tops, I came across the graves of 35 Confederates.... There was a Lieut. Col. buried along with them but there was no headboard to his grave." (How he knew the soldier was a "Lieut. Col" without a headboard is a mystery). Shortly afterward, perhaps in the fall of 1863, Dr. John O'Neal added Kearse to his compilation of Confederate burials, stating: "Lieut. Col. Kearse 50 Geo Jno. Roses Place orchard, near fence." Writing at another time, O'Neal lists the colonel as "Kearne," adding, "killed July 2; buried in the orchard, near the springhouse." In 1865, George Rose himself, using a waterstained notebook he had found on his property, recorded many of the identified graves dotting his land. On page five he wrote: "in the orchard near the springhouse Lt. Col Hearse 50 Ga."

Good, complete descriptions of the deaths of individual Southern soldiers during Civil War battles are quite rare among documents available to the modern day researcher. But as scarce as these accounts are, sightings of particular marked graves on battlefields are even more obscure. And finally, detailed de-

Col. Kearse's grave was near the springhouse which once stood in this area. (sch)

Grave of Lt. Col. Frances Kearse,
Laurel Grove Cemetery,
Savannah, Georgia. (rg)

pictions of the actual burials of the men are harder still to find. However, in the case of Francis Kearse, all three examples exist.

The death of Lt. Col. Kearse was witnessed by Sergeant William Jones of the 50th Georgia, late on July 2, when Semmes' Brigade "was called upon to take a battery located...in front of the enemy's line.... We advanced about two hundred yards," explained Jones, "when Col. Frank Kearse was killed by a grape shot, and soon afterward, Gen. [Paul J.] Semmes was shot in the thigh, from which it is said he bled to death." A member of Company B, 2nd Lieutenant William F. Pendleton added more, saying in his memoirs:

> About four in the afternoon we formed in line of battle behind a stone fence which was behind a hill. I knew a battle was imminent. Colonel Kearse addressed each company, telling the men to fight and win. Soon the firing from my brigade began.... We moved forward over a hill into an open field where we were under fire. We came to a road [Emmitsburg] with high fences on both sides; the fire was getting hotter. I wondered if I would ever get across the fences. We were going toward a peach orchard, but were ordered to right oblique. The firing was very heavy and dangerous. Colonel Kearse and Sergeant Hersey [sic] were killed. I didn't know it at the time, but both were killed dead.

At about 10 p.m., long after the fighting had ended, Lt. Pendleton, along with the rest of the 50th regiment, was pulled back to the brigade's position near the spring, north of the Rose house. On the way to the rear, walking under a moonlit sky, Pendelton asked another officer about the condition of Col. Kearse and was told of his death.

The following morning the lieutenant remembered that, "we gathered up the dead and buried them." Pendleton took a special interest in the disposition of the remains of his 26-year-old colonel. "I found a blanket on the field and we buried Colonel Kearse in it. I covered his face with an old shirt. During the burial I heard the battery start firing, so I went back to [our] position after marking Kearse's grave."

In the end, the marking of the gravesite with a crude wooden headboard enabled the lieutenant colonel to receive what all soldiers hope for—a proper and permanent burial. In 1871 Francis Kearse's bones were disinterred from the ground near Mr. Rose's springhouse and shipped to Laurel Grove Cemetery in Savannah, where he was reburied on September 24. There, in Lot Number 853, Grave Number 14, you can stand over Kearse's remains and pay tribute to his bravery and dedication. He fills his last resting place among other heroic comrades who lie,

> "Where the blades of the grave-grass quiver,
> Asleep in the ranks of the dead!"

TO DIE WITHOUT KNOWING

Sergeant Travis R. Maxey,
Co. K, 8th Georgia Infantry
Anderson's Brigade, Hood's Division, Longstreet's Corps

It is only natural to have some favorite characters, even in a book which delves into a topic repulsive to most people. The attraction which pulls toward the stories of a few of these individuals is too strong to ignore. One of those unexplained connections occurred for me, here, in the account of Orderly Sergeant Travis Maxey.

There are several reasons why this is so. In the first place, Maxey's complete name and rank were unknown when the research for this piece began. His "Combined Service Record" located in the National Archives, listed him simply as "T. R." This was a small thing certainly, but Maxey's complete history in that file reads as follows: "Maxey, T. R.—1st Corporal May 15, 1861. No later record." This notation, or lack thereof, is more serious, because the *sergeant* had offered up his very "person" to his new country. That valuable offering was accepted, then taken away in battle, but no remembrance, and no transcript of that sacrifice was ever made. Therefore, in a way, Travis Maxey was absent at the most important moment of his life. In the end, it would take a comrade of the sergeant's to rectify the matter. In this way, T. R. Maxey was given back his proper place in history.

The men who knew Travis Maxey best would always remember something he told them. It was a "desire" he had formulated, and it concerned the prospect of his death. Maxey's "wish" was later expressed by former Confederate Captain John C. Reid in a memoir he composed long after the events had passed. In it Reid explained: "Trav was the orderly sergeant of Company K. He had often said that if he was to be killed in the war, he wanted to be torn in pieces and die without knowing what had done it."

The second of July at Gettysburg was a terrible day for the rank and file members of the two armies who battled there from late afternoon until well into the night. The infantrymen of the 8th Georgia were no exception. For several long hours this regiment of 300 fought against Federal units holding the southwest section of John Rose's wheatfield. In these deadly encounters, nearly 170 Georgians from the 8th became casualties. One of them was Sergeant Maxey, a fact that might be unknown even today, had it not been for the memory of John Reid.

Among the first experiences the former captain remembered was the advance of his regiment, at "the double-quick" across an open field. Reid, then a lieutenant, was in his proper place behind the left of Company I. While traversing this ground, a shell detonated with a "stunning explosion" directly in the ranks to Reid's left. Immediately he saw the shirt of Sergeant Jefferson F. Copeland turn red. Lieutenant Reid was sure Copeland had been wounded, but that was not the case, as both men kept together, running for the protection of a wooded area ahead. There, under cover of the trees, which blocked only some of the artillery fire, the Confederates and their blue-coated enemies became locked in mortal combat. Reid said that the Southerners slowed their pace in his sector due to a deep bog almost 30 yards wide; it caused the attack to falter and the men to seek firing positions.

During the action at the bog, Reid was shot on the inner side of his right knee. Eventually, he reached the relative safety of the rear, but to do so, he had to hobble slowly along through a shower of musket balls which Reid was sure were searching for him personally. Coming upon the shelter of a slight depression in the earth, the injured lieutenant stopped under an apple tree, its branches shading a "large concourse of wounded friends."

There he found Sergeant Jeff Copeland, and he asked him how so much blood had come to soak his uniform. According to the sergeant, the blood was from Travis Maxey. "[T]he shell must have exploded inside of his body," said Copeland, "as his neck, head, and the upper part of his chest were all gone, and he could be recognized only by his clothes."

To the men present during this unplanned battlefield meeting, it must have seemed as if Sergeant Maxey's simple but bizarre wish had come true.

HE HAD COURTED DEATH

Private James Ouzts,
Co. K, 14th South Carolina Infantry
Perrin's Brigade, Pender's Division, Hill's Corps

This is a story of two soldiers whose lives may have been dissimilar in many ways, but whose deaths were closely intertwined. The men were Private James Ouzts and Captain William T. Haskell.

Haskell, who became a company commander in the 1st South Carolina Infantry, was born into a wealthy and influential family in 1837. By all accounts he was a man and officer of the highest caliber, and was greatly regarded by his comrades in the Confederate army. He had so far passed safely through every engagement with his regiment, and when, just prior to the invasion of the North in June 1863, the sharpshooters of Pender's Division were organized into a new battalion, Captain Haskell was chosen to lead it.

During the second day of the Battle of Gettysburg, Colonel Abner Perrin ordered Haskell's Battalion, with a few other troops from his brigade, to clear the enemy from a "dirt road" or lane that ran parallel to their position east of Seminary Ridge. This narrow and "sunken" road was west of the Emmitsburg Road, with Cemetery Ridge out to the east. The advance was successful, and after the sharpshooters took possession of the lane, Captain Haskell was seen "walking along the front line of his command, encouraging his men and selecting favorable positions for them to defend."

Obviously, Union infantrymen on Cemetery Hill and along the ridge southward were not going to let such an exposed enemy officer live very long. According to Colonel Perrin, the "virtuous, noble and accomplished" Haskell soon fell from "a wound from which he died in a few moments on the field." The colonel spoke of the able captain as an officer with "excellent judgement and a soldier of the coolest and most chivalrous daring."

Weeks later, when the mail arrived in the Abbeville District of South Carolina, informing William Haskell's mother of his fate, it also contained letters from the army giving the sad intelligence that her second son, Charles, and her brother Langdon Cheves had also died.

From all of the sources which describe Captain Haskell's character, his life and death, and the respect he held in Perrin's Brigade, there is no question that he was mourned and would be greatly missed by family, friends and military companions. But for one young soldier, the loss of William Thompson Haskell must have been even more keenly felt. In a company history of the 14th South Carolina written 32 years after the war, the depth of brotherly love and devotion shown by that 19-year-old comrade is made perfectly clear:

> In the second day's fight Company K lost one man, "Limber Jim Ouzts," killed with the sharpshooters of the brigade. He was a gallant soldier and devotedly attached to Captain Wm. Haskell,... and often said he would die for Captain Haskell if it was necessary. Captain Haskell was killed in the morning of the 2d, and Ouzts seemed to be regardless of fear after Captain Haskell's death, and fought with desperation as if to avenge the death of his fallen chief. Often during the day his splendid shots were noted by his comrades, and late in the evening he was killed almost instantly. He died without a struggle, with a smile on his face, as if he had courted death to be again with his Captain, who he knew could not come back to him.

According to a fellow officer, William Haskell's corpse was "left...buried near the scenes of his last exploits." In November 1866, ex-Confederates from his old unit located the grave and returned its moldering contents to the captain's native town. Upon arrival, his remains were met by the "survivors of the old company with which he had originally entered the service," and after a solemn ceremony, they were interred in the cemetery adjacent to the Episcopal Church.

By way of comparison, when James Ouzts was killed, his body probably did not receive the same treatment as that of his beloved commander. Ouzts' name is absent from all post-war burial registers, a fact that, from what little is known of his personality, may not have bothered him very much. So it is unknown whether he received a proper burial at the hands of his cohorts. If a burial was made, the grave either soon disappeared, or subsequently lost its marker. No one, not even Dr. O'Neal, made a notation of its location. And when in the spring of 1871, Dr. Rufus B. Weaver exhumed 84 South Carolinians from the Gettysburg battlefield and hospital areas, "Limber Jim" Ouzts was not among them. Therefore his remains did not travel to Charleston, and were not reinterred at the city's Magnolia Cemetery on May 10, with the others. But the words of Rev. Dr. J. L. Girardeau, in the patriotic address he gave that day, would still have pertained to the memory of James Ouzts, even though the private's bones were not present on the occasion the speech was delivered:

> Here let them sleep.... Shoulder to shoulder they stood: now let them lie side by side. Confederates in life, Confederates let them be in death.

If not in body or in spirit, but in memory alone, Jim Ouzts is, at least, now with his captain forever.

WON'T YOU TURN ME OVER?

Lieutenant Frederick Bliss,
Co. B, 8th Georgia Infantry
Anderson's Brigade, Hood's Division, Longstreet's Corps

For Emma M. Bliss, hundreds of days had passed since her son left home for the war in May 1861. Through all those long months, Lieutenant Bliss' widowed mother would never have become comfortable with the everyday strain of waiting for word of his status. The fear and worry must have been present day in and day out, as she ran her boarding house in Savannah. And if she had been near her son on the afternoon of July 2, as he stood bravely in the line of battle, Emma Bliss' worst fears would have been realized.

When Fred Bliss left for the army he was 21, and employed as a clerk in a commission house. Military duties would not have seemed unusual to Bliss, for he had been a member of a local militia company called the Oglethorpe Light Infantry since 1856. Described as "a gentleman, gallant and brave," Frederick Bliss, by 1863, had made a special friend of George Hillyer, a captain in the 9th Georgia, also of Anderson's Brigade. Hillyer and Bliss became acquainted when Hillyer had helped to acquit the lieutenant of the false and unjust charge of "leaving the ranks" during a previous battle. "Often after this," said Captain Hillyer, "when on the march, he would get permission and leave his command, and walk by my side. I found his presence and talk charming, and his sentiments noble."

On that second of July during the Battle of Gettysburg, Anderson's Brigade was in reserve within a wooded area along Seminary Ridge owned by a farmer named Biesecker. As other units of Hood's Division advanced and fought with the Federals between Rose's wheatfield and Little Round Top, the Georgia regiments under General Anderson waited for the order to attack. While the men rested, recalled Hillyer, Fred Bliss "came to where I was, and lying down on the clover, rest[ed] his head on my knee." Just then a soldier nearby pointed across the valley to the Yankee artillery and spoke up:

> Now boys, we are going to have a great battle and a great victory today. Suppose that...if some one of us would walk across that valley and up to those batteries and be blown to atoms by one of those cannon, and thus sacrificing one life instead of many the victory would be ours, is there one of us that could do it?

As Captain Hillyer began to examine his own mind to see if he was equal to such a grim task, he saw Lieutenant Bliss rise up, and with eyes beaming, point his finger to the enemy's guns, saying: "Yes if I could do that, I would walk straight across that valley and put my breast to one of the cannon and myself pull the lanyard."

In the assault that followed, Anderson's Georgians all took that long and deadly walk and battled the Northerners who held the ground between the Wheatfield and Devil's Den. This placed the 8th Georgia inside Rose's woods, and when they crossed a small brook which ran through the timber, enemy artillery fire "played havoc in their ranks." Among those struck, "in the heat of battle...fighting gallantly," was Frederick Bliss, who went down with a shattered knee.

Some two days afterward, on the afternoon of July 4, one of Lieutenant Bliss' comrades named Private Addison Tinsley, took a moment to write to the mother of another 8th Georgian who had been wounded on July 2. In that letter he also spoke of his lieutenant, explaining:

> Poor Fred Bliss died this morning about daylight. I saw him yesterday & was in hopes he would recover, & he appeared to think so; on returning to the "hospital camp" this morning I learned of his death. His right leg was amputated between the knee & body on the 3rd or perhaps the night of the 2nd. I think the former. I have a lock of his hair & a testament which I will send by first opportunity.

The hospital to which Frederick Bliss was taken was on the farm of Sarah and John Plank, which became the primary infirmary for Hood's Division. Bliss was placed on a cot in the Plank farmhouse where he "succumbed to shock and loss of blood" following an amputation at the thigh. On July 3, Captain Hillyer spoke to the chaplain of the 8th regiment, a Reverend Mr. Flynn, who reported that after the operation Bliss was given an opiate so he could rest. The chaplain also gave Hillyer an account of the lieutenant's last moments, which the captain disclosed:

Just before day the next morning he awoke out of his sleep, and Mr. Flynn, standing by the bed, Bliss apprehending fully where he was, spoke of his desperate wound and coming death. Lying on his side he asked Mr Flynn which way was the battle field. Mr. Flynn answered and pointed across his body to give the true di-

Grave of Lt. Frederick Bliss, Laurel Grove Cemetery, Savannah, Georgia. (rg)

rection. Bliss said, "Won't you turn me over?" They did as he requested and then he calmly said, "I did not wish to die with my back towards the field of battle."

Toward the autumn of that year, as the weather turned cooler in Pennsylvania, the thoughts of one of Fred's closest friends turned to Mrs. Emma Bliss, Fred's mother in Savannah. Still feeling sad about her, Lieutenant Sanford Branch, a wounded prisoner of war lying in the U. S. general hospital in Gettysburg, wrote these rugged sentiments home to his own mother, Charlotte: "Poor lady how I do sympathys with her. Fred was her darling boy, she almost worshiped him. he was a great loss to us, all ways kind & oblidging. he had meny meny friends but not a single enemy."

Branch also realized that having her son's body nearby would be a great comfort to Mrs. Bliss. Therefore, with the help of a Baltimore nurse named Melissa Baker, he arranged to have Frederick's body removed from the Plank farm and shipped to Georgia. The removal accomplished, the box containing his remains was addressed to Fort Monroe, Virginia. From there, it was to be placed into the care of the Southern express firm of *Thomas A. Bulkley and Company*, which would then forward it by "flag of truce" to Richmond, and eventually to Savannah.

But Lieutenant Branch worried that there would be complications in this move, and later, after making the arrangements, he confided to his mother: "Dear Dear Fred, how I should like to take charge of his body. I am so afraid something will happen to it. it would be dreadful if it should be lost." Unfortunately Branch was correct, and due to wartime restrictions, the plan did not succeed and the box was never released to Mr. Bulkley. Frederick Bliss' remains were kept for the remainder of the war somewhere in storage, probably in Baltimore under the care of Melissa Baker.

In June 1865, Baker wrote to Charlotte Branch inquiring as to whether or not Mrs. Bliss wanted Fred to be buried in Baltimore or sent to Savannah. About a month later word arrived from Emma Bliss to Melissa Baker; the remains should go to Georgia in the fall. But it took longer to complete this transfer that would finally bring comfort to Fred's mother. In February 1866, the shipment finally arrived in Savannah. There, on the 9th day of the month, in Laurel Grove Cemetery, Lieutenant Fredrick Bliss' bones were covered in the soil of his native state.

And close by him, in nearby graves, scores of other Confederates lay in ranks, silent and cold, keeping him company into eternity.

> Son, brother, patriot, friend. Sweet be thy rest,
> In thee Death claimed our bravest and our best.
> Content to fall, thy sole regret was this,
> To die without thy much beloved Mother's kiss.

I AM PREPARED

Private Archibald Y. Duke,
Co. C, 17th Mississippi Infantry
Barksdale's Brigade, McLaw's Division, Longstreet's Corps

It was sometime past noon on July 2 when Barksdale's Mississippians reached their battlefield post on "the enemy's front," a couple of miles south of Gettysburg, and just west of the Emmitsburg Road. Ahead of their position eastward a few hundred yards, and along the road, was a peach orchard, and nearby stood the barn, outbuildings, and brick house of Mary and Joseph Sherfy. Upon their arrival, a skirmish line was thrown forward, and due to the close proximity of the Federals, the men were told to lie down. One of the companies so deployed was "C," under Captain Gwin R. Cherry of the 17th Mississippi. Two members of Company C were brothers and privates, James W. and Archibald Y. Duke.

While in this exposed place, General James Longstreet rode up and ordered Captain Cherry to send two men to the Sherfy place, "without guns or cartridge boxes," to tear down the picket fences which stood around the yard and garden areas. The captain immediately notified his orderly sergeant to call out the first two names on the duty roster. This was done, but no one answered. Then the next two soldiers were called upon, and they also failed to get up. Angry and exasperated, Cherry emphatically stated, "I *will* make the detail," and added, "Jim Duke and Woods Mears, they will go." And go they did. But on the way to that very dangerous assignment, Duke turned to Mears and announced, "We will be killed."

But happily, as Duke and Mears worked quickly to pull down the palings, which were fifty paces from "three lines of infantry," no Yankee fired upon them. When they returned, Jim Duke noticed that Longstreet was still standing with the skirmishers. The general asked Duke, "Buddie, what did you see there?" Duke, who was dreading the expected attack, reiterated what he had seen, then posed his own question: "General, do you think we can take those heights?" And Longstreet replied, "I don't know, do you?" But before he received an answer, the general spoke again: "This is not my fight."

At about 4 p.m. the brigade was finally called to arms. Ten men from each company were then directed to the ordnance wagons to draw twenty rounds of extra ammunition for every man going into action. James and Archibald Duke were part of this contingent. As they made their way to the rear, Jim Duke had a talk with his sibling. And in 1906, he recalled for posterity the essence of their conversation:

73

[Archibald]... said he wanted me to write home after the fight. I replied that it was his time to write, as I had wrote last. [It was then that] I saw tears in his eyes. He said to me: "Something is going to happen to-day." I think my brother had a presentiment that he would be shot. In the first charge in the famous old peach orchard he was wounded, but I did not know of it until night. Our adjutant, Lieut. [John] Ansley, told me where he fell. I hunted until I found him. His first words to me were: "Thank God! my prayers are answered. I have asked him to take me in place of you, as I am prepared and you are not."

...[T]hat is the first time that I ever weakened. I promised him there that I would live a better life in the future, but it was many years before I did. His leg was amputated, but he lived several weeks. Gangrene in the wound caused his death. He died happy, so our chaplain wrote me. I am trying to meet him over the river.

When James Duke was writing his experiences of Gettysburg, 43 years had come and gone since the events had occurred. And from the little James wrote, it is uncertain if he knew any more about what happened to Archibald except what was told to him by the aforementioned chaplain. However, some additional information can currently be added to those facts.

First, it is known that after being injured, Duke was eventually taken by ambulance to a farm over two miles back on Marsh Creek, then owned by John S. Crawford. That farm became the field hospital of Barksdale's Brigade, but it may have been employed by other Confederate units as well. Medical personnel on duty there consisted of 27 nurses and cooks, plus several surgeons, and one chaplain, William B. Owen of the 17th Mississippi. A source identified Dr. F. W. Patterson in charge of the facility, and his assistants were Drs. R. L. Knox and C. H. Brown. This medical station was in service for about five or six weeks.

It was during this time that Archibald Duke died, and Chaplain Owen probably wrote the letter to James. That letter may have survived, and could perhaps give a description of Archibald's last days and his burial site, but it is not available. What is known, is that Gettysburg physician John O'Neal visited Crawford's farm on at least two occasions; and he was followed by Dr. Rufus B. Weaver.

Both men left bits of information about the burial and removal of A. Y. Duke's body. O'Neal merely lists Duke as having been interred "at Crawford's, on Marsh Creek," lying next to a soldier of Georgia's "Troup Artillery." Dr. Weaver was more specific. While working on the collection of Confederate remains in 1872, he found over 40 skeletons on that farm. Writing on one page of the register, he recorded: "The above Seven [remains] were buried on [the] North side of Mr Crawfords Walnut Avenue, on Marsh Creek, 4 miles S. W.

of Gettysburg. There were ten buried at this place. I exhumed nine—the tenth grave was empty— [William] Bigger's (I shipped him to Georgia to his brother last summer)."

Private Duke, and the eight others, along with the balance of the 40 to 45 Southerners at Crawford's, plus hundreds more from the fields and woods and meadows on and surrounding the battlefield, were transported in Dr. Weaver's "2nd Shipment" to Hollywood Cemetery in Richmond on August 2, 1872.

James Duke may or may not have had any of these facts concerning the final disposition of his brother's body. However, it is fairly certain that when James eventually went to his own grave, he had the satisfaction of knowing that Archibald had been accepting and comfortable in the knowledge of his forthcoming death, and more consequentially, he had been willing to die in James' place.

ALONE WITH THE DEAD

Private William S. Booton,
Co. A, 8th Georgia Infantry
Anderson's Brigade, Hood's Division, Longstreet's Corps

The war was only in its 37th day when William Sinclair Booton committed his fortunes to the "Rome Light Guards" on May 18, 1861. This company soon became "A," of the 8th Georgia Regiment of Volunteers. Although he had been born in Virginia on November 9, 1838, William Booton had moved from Madison County of that state to Rome, Georgia in his 21st year. And it was in that city that Booton decided to cast his lot with the new Confederacy, itself only a few months old.

By June 1861, Private Booton was once again on his native soil when his regiment traveled to the vicinity of Richmond to bolster the army of General Joseph E. Johnston. Engaged at First Manassas in July, Booton survived to fight on other fields of the Seven Days' Battles, including Mechanicsville and Gaines's Mills. But on Saturday, June 28, 1862, near Cold Harbor, his military fortunes took a decided turn for the worse. A bullet from a New Yorker's musket hit Booton in the thigh, causing a severe wound which placed William on injured furlough until September 7, 1862.

Back to duty in time for the Battle of Antietam, William Booton's diary entry for September 17 reads:

> Fight raging, we are...south of Sharpsburg. Gen. [Robert] Toombs wounded. Again we have met the 33rd New York regiment, the third time we have come in contact. I was shot by one of them near Richmond. The boys say not many of them left, we have almost demolished them.

True, but, ironically, at that very time, the 8th Georgia itself mustered less than 150 men.

During the Maryland Campaign, Private Booton's status as an infantryman changed, possibly due to the injury he had sustained three months earlier. He was reassigned to the brigade staff as clerk or secretary to General G. T. Anderson, a post he held until the very day of his death.

Eight months later in June 1863, Anderson's Brigade together with the whole of Lee's Army of Northern Virginia, began its second campaign into the Northern states. At one stage of this march, William consigned these sentiments to his diary: "Where we go next, time will tell and who can doubt we will ultimately gain our independence and an honorable peace outside of the once glorious but now contemptible union."

At Gettysburg, the forward movement of Lee's forces came to an abrupt standstill. The ensuing fight, a gigantic tug of war, became for each side a moment where, militarily and politically, much could be forfeited or gained. For William Booton personally, Gettysburg was the place where everything was lost.

Throughout the first day's fighting and into the second, Booton remained safely in the rear and on the march with General Anderson's headquarters staff. When General John B. Hood prepared his division for the upcoming combat, as part of Longstreet's advance against the Union left flank on the late afternoon of July 2, William's old company, the "Rome Light Guards" stood ready to enter the fray, with three officers and only 21 men.

At that juncture Private Booton, according to a member of his family, felt "impelled by a stern sense of duty and pure patriotism" to re-enter the ranks as a foot soldier. He applied to General Anderson for permission, which was at first denied. William asked again, and this time the request was granted. He quickly "grasped a rifle from a weary, foot-sore soldier, [who] was dragging himself along, and promptly fell in with his comrades."

Booton's life after that moment was short-lived. In the attack through the Rose farm woods, one of the first enemy shots to strike the 8th Georgia hit William. He died instantly, "surrounded by many relatives and friends," one of whom "leaned over his form, caught up his watch, gathered the few mementoes from his pocket, cut a lock of hair to tenderly bring back to the grief stricken ones at home, then obeying the sad order to 'fall back' left him alone with the dead."

An officer who had served with William in Company A, 2nd Lieutenant R. T. Fouche, afterward had this to say of his companion. "My association with Will was one of the most intimate character and I knew him well. His thoughts were pure and chaste, his deportment always dignified and gentle, his manner affable, but with it all he had the unflinching courage

The Confederate remains which were taken to Richmond, lay here in Hollywood Cemetery. (twh)

of a Lee. When he fell his family lost a jewel, his country a hero." Another man in the 8th, 1st Lieutenant Charles M. Harper, added this: "[William] was one of the most modest men I ever knew, and one of the most popular in the regiment."

And so died William Booton, one of so many "gallant youths in the budding of brilliant manhood" who were lost to the South forever. Family tradition has it that a Virginia cousin returned to the battlefield to the spot where William fell, but was unable to locate the body among the scores who had already been buried there. And supporting this story are all of the available Confederate burial rosters; none list Booton on any of their pages. Therefore, his remains were left, indeed, all "alone with the dead."

> Only a private! there let him sleep.
> He will need no tablet nor stone
> For the mosses and vines o'er his grave will creep
> and at night the stars through the clouds will peep
> And watch him who lies there alone!

THE OBJECT OF INTENSE AFFECTION

Lieutenant John Caldwell,
Co. E, 33rd North Carolina Infantry
Lane's Brigade, Pender's Division, Hill's Corps

The battle could not have been over long, when Adjutant and 1st Lieutenant Charles W. Cowtan of the 10th New York Battalion left the Union lines along Cemetery Ridge and walked down toward the Emmitsburg Road, barely 200 yards away. His path through this part of the contested ground was strewn with the corpses of Southerners of Heth's and Pender's Divisions, who had been killed on July 3 in the attack on General Hays' Federals of Meade's army.

But those were not the only dead to be seen. Out beyond the road and toward a farm lane 550 yards further still, were more bodies and scattered military debris from the intense skirmishing which had taken place on the afternoon of July 2 and the following morning. Somewhere in this bleak, death-haunted landscape, Adjutant Cowtan stooped down and retrieved a tattered and bloodsplattered document. The ragged paper turned out to be a Confederate lieutenant's commission made out to John Caldwell of North Carolina. How it got there is worth retelling.

John Caldwell, called "Jack" by his army comrades, was just sixteen when the Civil War began in 1861. He was the only son of an old and honored, as well as prosperous, family living in Morganton, North Carolina. John's father, Tod R. Caldwell, fairly doted on the handsome young man, who was described as the "object of intense affection." By the winter of 1862-63, John was determined to join the army, and the entreaties of his parents to do otherwise were of no consequence. So permission was granted, and the 18-year-old fulfilled his wish. On May 3, 1863, John enlisted, and was immediately appointed second lieutenant; the commission which announced the proud event was tucked securely away in his pocket, a prized possession to show his mother and father at the first opportunity. But that occasion would never arrive, because for eight years after the battle of Gettysburg, the exact disposition of John Caldwell himself remained a mystery.

Soon after the Battle of Gettysburg, a letter was directed to Tod Caldwell by Colonel Clark Avery of the 33rd regiment. It was dated July 18, 1863, and his words unintentionally gave the family the impression that John could still be alive. (Although a person reading Avery's words would have to be feeling desperate to think so.) Locating the whereabouts of young Caldwell evolved into something of an obsession, and according to one source:

[His father] used all the influence of money and position to find the lost soldier, but of course, to no avail. To the family, it could not be ascertained whether he was dead or alive, and the matter became one of terrible uncertainties. Finally, under the long strain of worry, the minds of the father and mother were nearly overcome. The father grimly nursed his great sorrow; he forbade any one to mention his son's name, and so the terrible possibilities were never alluded to, even by the mother.

Finally in 1871 the complete story of Lt. Caldwell's death and burial came to light. In that year Tod Caldwell was elected governor of North Carolina, and one day he was visited by a legislator from Hyde County named Wilson H. Lucas. Lucas was an ex-Confederate who had served as a lieutenant in Company F, of the 33rd Regiment. Just the evening before, Lucas had heard the sad account of the missing John Caldwell. He immediately went to see the governor, and gave him for the first time, the precise details of his son John's last hour of life. After hearing what Lucas had to say, Governor Caldwell "locked himself in his room all day, in tears." However, for some strange reason, the governor never revealed this information to his wife. In the end, she had to find out the facts through the efforts of the aforementioned New York lieutenant and adjutant, Charles Cowtan.

Why Charles Cowtan picked up Caldwell's bloody commission that day in 1863, is not known. But one thing is certain—he kept it for 24 years as a cherished relic of the Battle of Gettysburg. Then sometime in late 1887, Cowtan, who resided in New York City, contacted a newspaper correspondent in Raleigh, North Carolina, to find out if the reporter would assist in locating the family of the officer in question, in order that the document might be returned.

When the article about the lost commission was printed, one of the readers who saw it was Wilson Lucas. He quickly sent a letter to an attorney, Mr. J. B. Neathery, whom he hoped would find Mrs. Caldwell, and deliver to her a full narrative of her doomed son's experience and demise at Gettysburg. This letter was dated December 9, 1889, at Middleton, North Carolina, and was as complete a story as she could hope for:

Dear Sir

I know all about the death of Jack Caldwell. I stated the whole matter to Gov Caldwell in 1871. I will state them to you and you can communicate them to his mother. On the day of the 2nd of July 1863 We were in line of battle on Seminary ridge to the right and not very far from a Theological Seminary. Genl. [William D.] Pender who commanded our Division came up to Col. C M Avery who commanded our Regt. which was the 33rd N. C. State Troops and asked Col. Avery if he could pick out 75 men from his Regt with two officers who could take a certain point in a road in our front that was held by some Federal troops. Col. Avery told Genl. Pender we could and at once had 75 picked men formed in a line, and placed

Lt. W. H. Lucas knew the exact details of John Caldwell's death.

(sch)

in command of those 75 picked men were Lieuts Caldwell and myself. We were both 2nd Lieuts[,] but my commission being the oldest I was senior Lieut and put in command with Lieut Jack Caldwell as my assistant. We were brought up in a line in front of Genl. Pender who addressed me in these words (Can you take that road in front) I told him I did not know whether I could or not. At that reply he Genl. Pender seemed a little angry. And said to me if you can't take it say so and I will get some one who can. That touched me up and I replied to him, We can take it if any other 75 men in the Army of Northern Virginia can. Genl. Pender remarked that is the way I love to hear you talk. [H]e told us to hold our fire as long as possible but be sure and take the road. We formed the men in a line. I commanded the right and Lieut Caldwell the left. We had to charge through an open field with no protection whatever and our army on Seminary ridge could see the whole fight. We got within two hundred yards of them [and] we charged with a yell. And they stood their ground until we were within ten steps of the road. Then a part of them ran but 26 surrendered. And the very last time they fired upon us which was not more than twelve or 14 feet from them they shot Lieut Caldwell in the left breast. I did not see him fall. As soon as we were in the road one of the men told me Lieut Caldwell was killed. I went at once to the left and found him lying partly on his back and side, he was within 12 feet of the road. I called two men and we placed him on his back and spread an oil cloth over him[,] he was warm and bleeding very freely when I got to him. I could not send him out to the Regt for it was such an exposed place. The Federal skirmishers would kill a man before he could get a hundred yards.... We had 12 men killed and wounded out of the 75. It was the hottest place for a little while I was ever in during the war. Lieut Caldwell and myself were very fast friends. I loved him and I love his memory today, he was one of the noblest young men I ever knew, he was as brave as a lion, his mother has a just cause to be proud of her true, genuine, chivalrous son. He was not only beloved by the officers of his Regt but his men loved him devotedly. I had several of them weep bitterly when they were told of his death.... After night I had Lieut Caldwell placed upon a stretcher and carried to Seminary ridge where I [had] left the Regt[,] but they had moved.... So I buried Lieut Caldwell on Seminary ridge[,] I can go within a short distance of where he was buried.... There are two honey-pod trees close to his grave and he is buried not far from an old two story house. There are 7 graves near him those seven graves are the men that were killed in the charge with him. And those I think are the only graves near where he is buried. This statement is about as plain as I can make it to you.

I am very truly yours &c
W. H. Lucas

The area where the 33rd North Carolina Regiment was deployed before Lieutenant Lucas charged the "road," was near the David McMillan farmhouse, which is undoubtedly the "two story house" Lucus described. As to the gravesite of John Caldwell, the location was never recorded during or after the war, and its exact whereabouts remain a mystery. Examining Dr. O'Neal's burial registers for the fall of 1863, October 1864, and May, 1866, there are literally no members of the Thirty-third listed. Additionally, Caldwell and none of the other seven casualties turned up in boxed shipments sent to Raleigh in 1871 or Richmond in 1872-73 by Dr. Weaver. What did become of these men?

The good news was that the Raleigh newspaperman was successful in his search for the long dead lieutenant's relatives; the battered commission was sent directly to the still grieving mother. In thanking the reporter for the courtesy, Mrs. Caldwell wrote that, "for years she cherished the hope that her son was alive in some [military] prison." In fact, she said, "all the prisons were searched for him, through the influence of [then] Governor... [Zebulon B.] Vance."

And yet a second benefit of Adjutant Cowtan's generous spirit was that John Caldwell's mother became aware of Wilson Lucas' visit to Governor Caldwell in 1871, and was finally made privy to the particulars about John's death.

The circle was now complete. In her communication to the Raleigh correspondent, Mrs. Caldwell remarked that the "blood-stained and torn parchment is all there is on earth to remind [me] of [my] dead son." A simple, fragile thing, really, but to a sad and broken mother, it represented her boy's entire life; his body, his personality, and it allowed the fond memories of him to become more tangible, and to last in her heart forever.

Yes, but he was mine, my only son.

THE DEATH OF ALL HER HOPES

Lieutenant Colonel John C. Mounger,
9th Georgia Infantry
Anderson's Brigade, Hood's Division, Longstreet's Corps

Age may or may not be a factor when it comes to the bold actions of soldiers in battle. The young are expected to be foolish and brave, while older men are thought to be more cautious. However, the fathers of heroic youth can also hold the sparks of patriotism and valor within their aged breasts. This premise is clearly proven in the case of John Mounger.

When the 50-year-old lawyer, John Clark Mounger, led his regiment into battle that day of July 2, 1863, they first had to cross nearly a mile of open ground under a deadly enemy fire. This accomplished, Colonel Mounger next maneuvered his men through John Rose's shot-torn woods, where finally, his regiment struck the Yankees head on along the edge of a ripened wheatfield. And all the while they advanced, the colonel's thoughts must have hovered between his present and pressing duties, and one very uncomfortable fact. There, within the ranks of his steadfast regiment, marched one of the last two sons he had left in the world. And John Mounger would have had good reason to be concerned about them, because his eldest boy Terrell had been killed only two months before in the Battle of Chancellorsville.

As the 9th Georgia marched east toward the Federals, it held the left most position in Anderson's Brigade. This placed it directly in the path of a destructive enfilading fire from U. S. artillery and infantry, stationed in a peach orchard and along a narrow lane to the north. And because General McLaw's Confederate division had not yet been ordered up in support, there was no one to cover their flank.

It was said of Colonel Mounger, who had been seriously wounded earlier in the war at Sharpsburg, that in combat, he frequently exposed himself to enemy missiles "with a total contempt of danger." He was no different on this Thursday in Pennsylvania. A captain of the 9th later remembered that Mounger was killed, "soon after the advance commenced, while leading the regiment with his characteristic gallantry." (Three months later Mounger was officially cited for his bravery on the Confederacy's "Roll of Honor.")

After the colonel's fall, Thomas J. Mounger helped to carry his dead father off the field. He was eventually interred with great care in a small family cemetery west of Gettysburg. The grave was dug close to a blacksmith shop, on the farm of Ephraim Whisler. By the fall of 1871 his remains had been removed, but up until that date they were described as being "in excellent order," a sure sign that someone who knew the colonel had done the burying.

On September 24, 1871, John Mounger was reinterred in Laurel Grove Cemetery, Savannah, Georgia, in Lot 853, Grave #14.

On or about July 15, the second son, Lieutenant John C. L. Mounger, wrote to his mother, Lucie, living in Quitman, Brooks County, in the extreme southern part of Georgia. An initial letter, which has been lost, had briefly imparted the news of her husband's death. Follow-up correspondence to Lucie Mounger outlined in more detail the facts concerning the disposition of the body. Fortunately this final letter survived, and is here presented nearly in its entirety. There is a startling revelation in the last few sentences, which undoubtedly made the death of Colonel Mounger all the more difficult for her to bear.

Camp near Martinsburg, Va
July 18, 1863

Dear Mother,

I wrote you a few days ago concerning the death of our *dear Father*, he was killed on the 2nd of July about an hour by the sun, he is buried in a family grave yard 1/2 miles below Gettysburg, [sic] Pennsylvania on the Chambers[burg] and Baltimore Turnpike. Captain [John] Sutlive had a good coffin made for him and we put him away as well as could be expected. I have the dimensions of his coffin, so when we get a chance to move him, we can get a box...for him without any trouble. Pa died very easy, Tom says. I was not with him when he died. I was detailed and sent off after cattle some three or four days before the fight. Tom took good care of *dear dear* Pa until he died, but he lived only a few minutes after he was shot. He was shot with a minie ball through the right breast and a grape shot from cannon through the bowels. Dear Mother, we tried to carry him to Virginia before we buried him, but it was impossible, as the Yankees were all around us and we could not get across the river without being captured. Dear Mother, let us all try to meet him in Heaven. Tom and myself will try and be better boys. Tom kept the stars on his coat and a lock of his hair. I wrote you a few days ago, but I was in so much trouble that I do not recollect what I wrote. Dear Mother, Pa has his horse here. I would like to know what to do with him, as I cannot draw feed for him. I can sell him, but he will not bring more than 3 or 4 hundred dollars in the condition he is in, and as for getting him home, it would be impossible. I will be able in a few days to send you One Thousand dollars ($1000) which will help you buy a place to live on....

Dear Mother, in my next letter, I will send you Pa's resignation which he wrote out before he went into Pennsylvania. He intended handing it in as soon as he returned to Virginia[,] and go home.

Tom and myself send our best love to you, Dear Mother....

Your affectionate sons,
John and Tom

What happened to John and Tom Mounger? Two members of their family were now dead, and the war was far from over. Did these two young men survive, and return to comfort their grief-stricken mother? Unfortunately, there would be no respite for Lucie Mounger. Before the end of the war came in 1865, her remaining sons had their own rendezvous with the "grim reaper." At the Battle of the Wilderness in early May 1864, both youths perished, doing their whole duty like their father before them. A historian of the regiment described the sad finale:

> As Lt. John Mounger of the 9th Georgia, Company H, knelt down to instruct his men on firing, he was shot in the head by a minie ball and died instantly. His brother, Thomas, continued the charge and reached the [enemy's] breastworks, only to be shot in the neck. He died a few minutes later.

A newspaper account of the action which claimed the lives of Mrs. Mounger's two boys, added more:

> Of the 9th Georgia, Captains [N. C.] Duncan and [William E.] Cleghorn were killed, Captain [Edward A.] Sharpe missing, and Lieut. Mounger and brother killed. The two latter are sons of Col. Mounger of the 9th who died at Gettysburg. Another son was killed at Chancellorsville, thus destroying the whole of this family, and leaving an aged lady to mourn over the death of all of her hopes.

Not for fame or reward, not for place or rank,
not lured by ambition or goaded by necessity;
but in simple obedience to duty as they understood it;
these men suffered all, sacrificed all, dared all, —
and died.

GOD HELP HER BEAR IT!

Captain Isaac D. Stamps,
Co. E, 21st Mississippi Infantry
Barksdale's Brigade, McLaw's Division, Longstreet's Corps

No one will ever know for certain who was the first Confederate soldier to have his remains exhumed from the battlefield of Gettysburg, to be returned home for final burial. But if a candidate had to be chosen, Captain Isaac Stamps would be very high on that list.

Isaac Davis Stamps was born in 1828 on Rosemont Plantation near Woodville, Mississippi, near the home of Jefferson Davis, who would eventually become the president of the Confederate States of America. Stamps' mother Luccinda, was Davis' sister. Isaac married Mary E. Humphreys in 1854, and they made their first home in New Orleans while he studied law. After his graduation, Mary and Isaac moved back to Woodville where he began his practice. The couple had four children, one of which died before 1861.

Soon after the war began, Isaac Stamps enlisted in the 21st Mississippi, and was immediately elected captain of Company E. Upon this significant occasion, his uncle, President Jefferson Davis, presented Isaac with the sword Davis had himself carried during the Mexican War almost fifteen years earlier.

It was not long before the 21st regiment was transferred to Virginia, where it began its long connection with what became known as the Army of Northern Virginia. During the early months of Isaac's service, the duties of military life kept him far from home. Meanwhile, Mary remained in residence at Rosemont, where in the spring of 1862, she lost a second child, Sallie. A year later, Mary and her surviving two girls traveled to Richmond to visit their relatives, President Davis and his wife Varina. During this interval, Captain Stamps, who was stationed only 50 miles away, secured a leave of absence and joined Mary in the Confederate White House.

While on this furlough, Isaac confided to Mary that he believed he would soon die in battle. He was so certain of this premonition, that he extracted a promise from Mary; when it happened, she must retrieve his body and return it to the family plot at Rosemont. Mary agreed, but with this acknowledgement, she certainly must have felt even stronger concern that Isaac might not survive the war.

Captain Stamps' premonition came to pass at Gettysburg on July 2. In the late afternoon, Barksdale's Brigade charged a Union held "salient" position around Joseph Sherfy's farm and peach orchard which straddled the Emmitsburg Road a few miles from Gettysburg. According to an eyewitness, Captain Stamps received a painful and mortal wound to his bowels just as the 21st Mississippi entered the western edge of the ripening orchard. As the furious battle raged around him, Stamps lay in agony out in the open, under a burning sun, until night fell and members of his battered regiment came to assist. While waiting for an ambulance, Mary's father, Benjamin Humphreys, the colonel of the 21st, sat with Isaac. There on the torn and bloody ground, and under the pale light of a summer moon, they talked for several hours.

On the morning of July 3 Captain Stamps was still alive. When transportation became available, he was carried westward about two miles to the brigade hospital established the day before on the farm of Gettysburg attorney John Crawford. But all too quickly, even before midafternoon, Captain Stamps slipped from life's tenuous bonds. In those last hours waiting for the end, he was attended to by Dr, George Peets of the regiment, who testified that Isaac's dying words were: "My poor wife! God help her bear it!"

In the days following the defeat at Gettysburg, Mary Stamps waited impatiently with President Davis' family in Richmond for news from her husband

and the army. As reports began to trickle in, her worse fears were confirmed. Isaac was gone; there was no doubt about it, especially when Surgeon Peets returned with the captain's sword, and gave Mary the particulars of his death and burial place.

There can be no doubt in our hearts that the next few weeks were terrible for Mrs. Stamps. But out of this tragedy, the third in her short life, came forth a determination to honor Isaac's last request. With the help of Jefferson Davis, Mary began to seek a way in which she could recover his body from enemy territory. The process was not an easy one; it became a long and difficult problem, as United States authorities were not then in favor of granting such requests, even through formal channels. Eventually, by November 1863, due to pressure from Union families wanting to recover their own deceased soldiers from Southern battlefields, an exchange was agreed upon. With permission in hand, 26-year-old Mary Stamps began the complicated and lengthy ordeal to get Isaac home.

The actual journey began in late November; altogether it took nearly two months, and when ended had covered over 1200 miles. Mary initially went from Richmond to City Point, Virginia, under a "flag of truce." Next her travels took her to Baltimore, and on to Gettysburg. In Pennsylvania she most likely hired Dr. John W. C. O'Neal, the Southern-born physician who had just completed a first ever compilation of approximately 1000 or more identified Confederate burials on or near the 25-square-mile battlefield. Probably with the good doctor's assistance, Mary found the name she sought, and lost no time in proceeding out to Crawford's place on the east bank of Marsh Creek. Surgeon George Peets had described to Mary the exact burial site, so when the wagon pulled up at Crawford's stone tenant house, Mary looked around for Isaac's grave, which should have been, in "a soft spot in a wheat-field under a medium sized oak." The wheat had long since been harvested, but on that bleak winter day, in a barren field not far from the house, stood a line of weathered wooden headboards sitting atop a few eroded earthen mounds. One of the markers read: "Capt. I. D. Stamps, Co. E, 21st Miss." At the sight of his name, Mary fell to the ground, momentarily blinded by tears.

On this day however, her time for crying was shortlived. Mary Stamps was a persistent and determined woman, and she knew that the real difficulties and discomforts of the task were only beginning. After a brief graveside visit, Mary returned to town and secured the services of an undertaker, who went out and exhumed the captain's body and settled it into a metal coffin. The cost of that coffin and the shipment to Richmond came to $133.70. Mary did not abandon her husband at this point. Instead, she accompanied his remains on the rail trip from Gettysburg to Baltimore, then aboard a "flag of truce" boat to City Point, and again on a railroad car to Richmond. Once in the capitol, she decided to continue the southward journey to Mississippi, writing to a relative: "I am now going to carry him to Woodville to the old home."

The last leg of this already tedious undertaking was by far the most frustrating. For the new widow, the train ride from Virginia through the Carolinas and Georgia was, due to the condition of the line during wartime, extremely slow and uncomfortable. Near Montgomery, Alabama, the railroad tracks were torn up, but that small setback did not deter Mary Stamps. She purchased a wagon, hired a driver and guard, and pushed on, sitting day after day next to Isaac's coffin, and sleeping on the ground at night, wrapped in his army cloak.

Rosemont Plantation, the long awaited destination, was reached in January 1864 on an overcast day, thus ending a 400 mile wagon ride, and the last leg of a sad, hard adventure. Soon, surrounded by family and friends, the dead officer was laid to rest next to his beloved daughter Sallie.

Six months before, Captain Stamps had fallen, a casualty in an enemy's land. But he had been able to come home. Isaac's strong, dedicated and loving Mary had faced for him almost impossible and insurmountable odds, simply to fulfill his wish.

And to keep the promise she had faithfully made.

SHOT DEAD IN HIS TRACKS

Private John E. Dixon,
Co. K, 3rd Georgia Infantry
Wright's Brigade, Anderson's Division, Hill's Corps

It seems inappropriate to profit from the death of another. Yet this is a common practice and happens repeatedly. In the strange story of John Dixon, this profiteering was indirect and accidental, and occurred on the battlefield of Gettysburg.

On the late afternoon of July 2, the brigade of General A. R. Wright was waiting its turn to be sent into action along a section of Seminary Ridge, near where the Virginia Memorial stands today. Eventually, as part of a Confederate assault against Federal units holding a line along the Emmitsburg Road, it would leave the ridge and participate in the general attack. But for the time being, the brigade, consisting of three Georgia regiments and one battalion, merely skirmished with the enemy in its front. During most of the day, Company K of the 3rd Georgia Infantry was detailed to this skirmish line. On that fateful afternoon, and in that particular company were four men, all friends, whose lives would intertwine in a most bizarre manner before the battle was over. They were Privates John E. Dixon and James O'Farrell, Sergeant Rufus K. Reaves, and Corporal James S. Parr.

The story of the death of one of these men, John Dixon, known as "Dixie" to his comrades in the 3rd regiment, really started on June 30, the day before the fight at Gettysburg. It seems that Dixon, a general favorite by all accounts, and "as gallant a man who ever followed the fortunes of the immortal Lee," appeared to be unusually disturbed on that Tuesday. Bothered by this anxiety, Dixon went to speak to his messmate Jim O'Farrell. In the conversation that followed, "Dixie" related how he was having a strong "presentiment that there would be a great battle soon, and that he would be killed early in the engagement." Knowing it was common for soldiers to have such feelings, (which almost never came true), O'Farrell laughed it off, and he and the other friends of Dixon, tried to make light of his superstition. But their attempts were of no avail, for nothing could shake "Dixie's" dread, and his low-spirited mood continued unabated.

It is not known for certain when or how Private Dixon was killed on July 2, but O'Farrell said he was one of the first to fall, "shot dead in his tracks." After nightfall, a squad was formed and led by James Parr for the purpose of burying the body. No one in that squad pinpointed the grave for future notice, but according to a list compiled after the battle by local physician John O'Neal, Dixon's grave was located south of Emanuel Pitzer's farmhouse "in the edge of the woods." (Near him were buried eight other Confederates, but by May 1866, Dixon's, plus four other graves had been obliterated.)

When the somber task was completed, Corporal Parr and another of Dixon's messmates decided to mark the site. Seeing a bake oven nearby, which was on the property of the Pitzer family, the two men thought they might find something suitable for a "headboard" among the stones used to build the structure. As Parr began to rummage around the flat rocks on the floor of the hearth, he heard a jingling sound, and, "striking a light discovered a pile of gold and silver, and a number of paper bills." Securing about $1200 worth, which was all he could carry, Parr took it to his regimental bivouac. Later, on his return for the balance of the treasure, he found it gone; someone had beat him to it. Since Parr was an infantryman, he asked R. K. Reaves, who as commissary sergeant was mounted, to carry the money back to Virginia. After counting it carefully "on the battlefield, by the light of their campfire," the men parted. When they were safely reunited across the Potomac River, Reaves turned over every cent to Parr, who somehow got it back to Athens, Georgia.

Corporal James Parr may have been considered by some of the citizens of Adams County, Pennsylvania, as a thief and a marauder, but to the Southern army he had the kind of soldierly record that would make the defeat of the Confederacy difficult. Specific details in his military file are scarce, but Parr, although wounded three times during the war, remained faithfully in service until he was paroled by the Federal army a few days following Lee's surrender at Appomattox Court House, Virginia. Jim O'Farrell, Parr's companion in this odd caper, confessed that the acquired wealth allowed Parr "to start himself in business after the war."

Was there really such a treasure hidden in an obscure bake oven on that Gettysburg farm? The answer is a definite yes. The farmer mentioned in this account, Emanuel Pitzer, was born in 1785 and was married to Philahena Degroft in 1844. He died exactly two weeks prior to the death of Private John Dixon, on June 18, 1863. Pitzer's neighbors later asserted that the old fellow "distrusted banks." From other sources, it is known that his son Samuel, age 48, was anxious for Emanuel's passing so he could collect the sizable inheritance of his father's 233 acre farm, and the hoarded cash. Unfortunately for Samuel, he chose the wrong place to secret the loot so recently obtained.

Consequently, Samuel's greed, and Private Dixon's untimely demise, gave rise to the discovery of the money. This in turn led Dixon's friend Parr, who was just another destitute Southern soldier, to a fresh start in 1865, and a new and prosperous life thereafter.

As the old saying goes, "all's fair in love and war."

I AM RUINED

Private Robert W. Crawford,
Co. B, 11th Alabama Infantry
Wilcox's Brigade, Anderson's Division, Hill's Corps

Late on the second day of the battle, the ranks of General Cadmus Wilcox's Alabama brigade were formed in readiness. They would soon participate in the general assault already in progress against units of the Army of the Potomac holding ground along the Emmitsburg Road from Sherfy's peach orchard to the Codori farmhouse west of Cemetery Ridge.

Later, in a letter written to his sister and mother from, "Camp 11th Ala. Regt. Near Bunker Hill, Va. July 17th 1863," Sergeant Fleming W. Thompson explained the next sequence of events. "[A]fter the Rebs got [the Yankees] started on the right they began to give way on the left, we heard the yell & could see them running." Then, as Wilcox's Brigade entered into the fray, Thompson said:

> [A]bout this time we was ordered to move to the front, we did not get far before we came in contact with them and as soon as we got near them, we were ordered to Charge which we did & drove the enemy about a mile or more, we broke & drove both their first and second lines of Battle, and when we got to their 3rd line which was in a very strong position...we was forced to fall back a half mile & rally....

It was then that Thompson noticed the serious injury to his friend, Robert Crawford. He wrote, "The loss of our Company...was one killed [John C. Ridgway] & poor Bob Crawford was mortally wounded[,] he was shot through the bowels with a musket Ball, it entered near his right hip in [the] bone....[W]hen the Ball struck him he threw his hand up to his breast and said boys I am ruined,...."

After the bullet hit Crawford, he walked about 100 yards back to a house, probably that of David Klingle, where he remained until the day's fight was over. As darkness approached, Sergeant Thompson went to the house and helped Crawford back to an aid station, staying with him until he was taken to the brigade field hospital. In his letter home, Thompson wrote that the bullet was cut out near Crawford's left hip joint, indicating a wound not easily repairable by even today's methods, but especially troublesome in 1863. Fleming Thompson further indicated to his family that Crawford knew he was mortally wounded, explaining that, "Bob... was willing to go as it had fallen to his lot,..." All that Private Crawford asked was for Thompson to write his "Papa" as soon as possible, and tell the family "he was not afraid to die." This Thompson did at Hagerstown, Maryland. He also kept the bullet that killed Crawford, in order to present it to Robert's people if they desired the memento.

The field hospital of Wilcox's Brigade was southwest of Gettysburg and north of the Fairfield Road on the farm of Nancy and Adam Butt. When Bob Crawford died, he was given a decent burial. This befitted a soldier of Lee's army who had fought well, and radiated strength and bravery even to his last breath. The grave was south of Butt's stone farmhouse near the road, surrounded by about 25 deceased comrades from Anderson's Division. All of these remains were removed to Hollywood Cemetery in Richmond during the early 1870s. Private Robert Crawford was shipped in Box I-122.

He lies there now, buttressed on all sides by the remains of honorable men he was proud to know in life, and willing to join in death.

It was common practice to save the bullets that killed or wounded. Here a Union doctor sent home the ball that ended the life of Sgt. Wickliffe Kincheloe, 8th Virginia.

The Casualties Of Day Three: July 3, 1863

I RELIEVED HIS BODILY WANTS

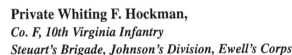

Private Whiting F. Hockman,
Co. F, 10th Virginia Infantry
Steuart's Brigade, Johnson's Division, Ewell's Corps

The Muhlenburg Rifles was a Shenandoah County, Virginia, company, first organized just five days after Fort Sumter fell to Southern guns on April 13, 1861. A 21-year-old Woodstock resident, W. F. Hockman, became a member of this unit on the same day. It could be said that he was one of the earliest Confederate volunteers. And two years and a little over two months later, Whiting Hockman was still in the ranks, as he stood in battle formation with his comrades on July 2, facing a ridge which ran from Culp's Hill to Spangler's Spring, just south of Gettysburg.

Sometime during the assault that followed, Private Hockman was shot twice through the lungs and once in an arm. Left behind, he became a captive of the same men who had tried to kill him. These enemy soldiers eventually carried Hockman to the field hospital of the U.S. 12th Army Corps, located on the farm of George and Anna Bushman along Rock Creek. The lower floor of the Bushman's barn held many of the 125 wounded Confederates quartered there. He may have lay in this building, or outside nearby with other injured "Rebel" prisoners of war.

Sometime between July 9-10, Hockman was accidently discovered by Charles Cort of Somerset, Pennsylvania, who had come to Gettysburg to assist some of the 22,000 injured left in the vicinity by the two departed armies. Charles Cort immediately recognized the young Confederate, for in the spring of 1862 he had met Whiting Hockman and his family in Woodstock, Virginia, while traveling with a Franklin and Marshall College (Lancaster, PA) classmate, M. H. Hockman, who was probably Whiting's brother. When Charles Cort first saw his old acquaintance, he felt a deep personal interest in the dying infantryman, and later wrote: "I relieved his bodily wants and ministered such spiritual advice as was necessary." Private Hockman was calm throughout, said Cort, and accepted the prognosis that his wounds were "necessarily fatal." Cort telegraphed Hockman's brother, a minister in Lancaster, Ohio. But it was already too late; within a few days, on July 15, W. F. Hockman died of his injuries.

Because he died on an organized Union hospital site, Pvt. Hockman's grave survived with eight other Southerners on Bushman's land until the early 1870s. At that time, all remains on the farm were collected and shipped to Richmond. Whiting's grave, which had been well marked by another family friend, E. H. Dieffenbacher, was part of the transfers. All burials had taken place in a field east of the main house. This hospital graveyard, remembered one Union soldier, was divided accordingly; "one half for the Blue and the other for the Gray."

The Hockman story survived through a strange collection of interesting coincidences. This young Virginian was shot down in battle in a country once his own. He was given aid and comfort in the waning moments of his life, on what was now foreign soil, from a man his family had befriended in peace, years earlier. His brother, living in the North, was kindly sent for to attend him in his dying hours. And in death, his grave was carefully marked by another friend, who should have been his enemy.

In a "Civil War," such things can happen.

A RECKLESS AND GALLANT SOLDIER

Sergeant William H. Prince,
Co. A, 5th Virginia Infantry
Walker's (Stonewall) Brigade, Johnson's Division, Ewell's Corps

If it were in my power, it would be satisfying to give each and every man who died at Gettysburg a few paragraphs, as it were, "of immortality." All soldiers who were lost in that tragic war should receive the same treatment. They all deserve it. But that cannot ever happen. For even the few who enliven these pages, "immortality" is at best a fleeting honor. In some cases too, the "immortality" is questionable, for the people discussed in the narrative may or may not be the actual soldier described in the account. Sergeant Prince falls into this category.

William Prince left his occupation as a shoemaker in Winchester on April 20, 1861, and enlisted as a private in the 5th Virginia Infantry at age nineteen. By the end of 1862, Prince had been promoted to sergeant, and was still serving in that capacity when his brigade entered into combat on Culp's Hill early in the morning of July 3. Prince's unit, the old "Stonewall Brigade," commanded at Gettysburg by General James A. Walker, started their fight at daylight. They attempted for several hours, with other regiments of Johnson's Division, to capture Federal defensive barricades which snaked along a ridgeline from McKnight's Hill, over Culp's Hill, and ended down near Spangler's Spring.

General Johnson's troops had been unsuccessful in a similar attempt the evening before, mainly due to the formidable earthen, log, and stone breast-works which had been constructed by the enemy along this high ground, and because of the merciless firepower they shielded. A few of Walker's men, especially from the 4th Virginia, got fairly close to their Yankee adversaries, but generally it was clear suicide to approach even to within 100 yards of those heavily fortified and well defended positions. By noon on Friday, July 3, the fight for Culp's Hill was over. Casualties in Walker's Virginia brigade reached 322 killed, wounded, and prisoners; not a catastrophic loss, considering the imbalanced nature of the contest, and the difficulties the terrain presented.

The engagement at Culp's Hill may have ended by midday on July 3, and the Battle of Gettysburg is generally accepted to have been over by the evening of the same day, but for one man of the "Stonewall Brigade," some unfinished business remained. The only record concerning this incident comes from Sergeant Lawrence Wilson, a member of the 7th Ohio Infantry Volunteers. This regiment had faced Walker's troops in combat more than twelve hours earlier. And Wilson had previously made it clear that the Confederates opposing the 7th Ohio's sector were indeed Virginians:

Grave of Sergeant William Prince, 5th Virginia Infantry, buried in Winchester, Virginia. (rg)

93

On the night of July 3, about midnight, when the battle having ended and the stillness was only broken by the moans of the wounded yet uncared for in our front, and when the men in the trenches, exhausted from days of marching and fighting, were sound asleep, a Confederate Sergeant made his way stealthily up to our works, and seeing our regimental flag, with staff, leaning against the logs, he reached up, and being much lower, as he stood on the slope of the hill on the outside, could not reach over the head log, so grasped the staff through the firing space underneath and began to work it up so that it would topple over and fall into his arms.

This movement awakened our color Sergeant, who sprang up in a dazed, drowsy condition and shot and killed this handsome, reckless, and gallant soldier in gray before he was fairly aware of it and much to the sorrow and regret of his [Southern] comrades when the facts became known. This shooting alarmed and aroused our line of battle, and supposing another attack was on, firing broke out afresh, but at daylight we could only find this lonely Sergeant as the cause and the only victim of the outbreak.

There were five sergeants from the "Stonewall Brigade" killed during the battle: Prince of the 5th Virginia, George Phlegar and Solomon Sexton of the 4th, and James Menifie and John Rosenberger of the 33rd. So then, why identify the soldier shot by the 7th Ohio as William Prince? The answer may lie in the way the dead were buried at Culp's Hill.

Starting on July 4, Northern soldiers began the unpleasant task of interring the U. S. dead within their own lines, and the corpses of the "Rebels" scattered eastward throughout the Confederate infantry positions sloping down toward Rock Creek. A member of the 149th New York recorded that all Union bodies were carefully placed in single graves and marked with appropriate wooden headboards, until, he said, "[i]n a short time the 2nd Division had quite an extensive cemetery of its own." Explaining further, this New Yorker wrote: "The enemy's dead, with a very few exceptions, were buried indiscriminately in long trenches dug near the spot where they fell." A civilian who lived nearby named J. Howard Wert, added that these trenches, (he counted seventeen), were generally far down from the breastworks and closer to the creek.

Therefore, the body of Sergeant William H. Prince possibly became one of the "few exceptions" noted above by the New Yorker. Counting *all* Southerners collected and interred in the vicinity of Culp's Hill, only two Confederates were given identified graves, or what could be termed, "exceptions." They were buried, "back [of] Culp's Hill, (or Raspberry Hill, as it was better known in 1863), in [the] woods near [the] Union graves."

One of these "Rebs" was an officer, a major on the staff of General Johnson. He was Benjamin Leigh, and had been shot very near the Yankee lines. Due to his notable bravery in the battle, Leigh was given special consideration when it came time to bury the dead. Therefore, it just stands to reason that if the

Federals admired the courage of the "Confederate Sergeant" who tried to capture their flag, and having his body right in their midst, they might do the same for him. And since he caught their attention, and was closer than any other enemy soldier, would they not have, out of mere curiosity, searched his pockets and attempted to discover who this daring man was? Then, out of respect and courtesy, might they have buried him nearby, identifying his grave as they had for Major Leigh? This happened often during the Civil War, as is attested to by the participants, and may be the only logical reason why only Sergeant Prince and Benjamin Leigh were the benefactors of uniquely marked graves adjacent to the Union cemetery.

> Under the sod, under the clay,
> Here lies the blue, there the grey.

When Dr. O'Neal was compiling his Confederate burial list in 1863, he indicated a gravesite for William Prince on "Raspberry Hill," with a notation that read "Removed." Subsequently, on O'Neal's 1866 register, Prince's name is not present. The reason for this disappearance is written in his military records. Sergeant Prince's remains were recovered and reinterred into Mt. Hebron Cemetery, Winchester, Virginia, probably between 1864 and 1866.

And as to whether or not it was Sergeant Prince who had the sheer audacity, boldness, and cool nerve to try for that Ohio battle flag, we will really never know. But in point of fact, and for some odd reason, Prince got special treatment from his enemies.

But the answer, it seems, is still buried with them all.

HIS DYING REQUEST

Private James M. Larew,
Co. E, 1st Virginia Cavalry
Fitzhugh Lee's Brigade, Stuart's Cavalry Division

All students of the Gettysburg Campaign are at least somewhat familiar with the activities of General J. E. B. Stuart's cavalry division's movements during the time period leading up to the renowned battle itself. There are usually two main viewpoints concerning these maneuvers. One supports the general's tactics; the other believes he committed serious mistakes which helped to push Robert E. Lee into the unintended involvement in a fight which he ultimately lost. But whatever the opinion, the facts cannot be altered: Stuart was not available when Lee needed him most. All of which leads to this story—a tale of two cavalrymen, who, partly due to General Stuart's decisions, did not survive the campaign into Pennsylvania.

In late June 1863, "J. E. B" Stuart broke off from directly protecting the main body of the Army of Northern Virginia, and marched part of his cavalry division eastward and then around the rear of the Union Army of the Potomac. After collecting intelligence on the disposition and movements of that powerful enemy force, Stuart's task was to immediately rejoin the marching columns of Lee's army, report his findings, and resume his real priority, which was to guard the Confederate right flank. But in his "ride around the Federals," Stuart's troops were cut off by the rapid northward advance of the Yankees. This unintended situation and other misadventures caused Stuart a delay in reaching Lee in time to prevent a premature collision with the Northern army. Stuart's off-course route, among other places, took him through Rockville, Westminster, Hanover, then up to Carlisle, and finally on to Gettysburg, where his troopers arrived on July 2, during the very middle of that sanguinary engagement.

Earlier, at Hanover on June 30, Stuart's Confederate horsemen had surprised a U. S. cavalry force under General Judson Kilpatrick. It was during that brief clash, that the personal side of this story starts to unfold.

After a late morning initial encounter, Kilpatrick's men rallied and quickly drove Stuart's cavalrymen, who were widely dispersed, out of the town. One of the troopers involved in this little scrape was Private Christian H. Koiner, of Company E, 1st Regiment, Virginia Cavalry. Sergeant Benjamin James Haden, Jr. of the same unit, was a witness to the events which transpired there. He explained:

> I had just dismounted to procure the arms and horse of a Yankee who had been wounded, when Billy McClausland...came back at full speed, telling me...[the Yanks] were charging us with heavy force. I knew when he left times were getting squally, so I mounted, putting the captured horse in front of me...and brought him out safely. We lost some good men in this charge; C. H. Koiner, of my company, had his horse killed while making the charge, and had mounted a Yankee's horse, (the rider of which had been killed) [Koiner] was shot, the ball passing through the front of the saddle and then through him, wounding him mortally. They pursued us until we reached our support and then retired.

Sergeant Haden was almost correct in his summation of Private Koiner's experiences. Koiner, then 20 years old, was a former carpenter and native of Augusta County. His army files show that after being wounded, he did not die immediately, but was instead captured and sent to the military prison at Fort Delaware, where he died of disease exactly two months later. Private Koiner's burial took place in New Jersey at what is now called the Finn's Point National Cemetery.

The sergeant does not say so literally, but it appears that after the Hanover action, another member of Haden's company acquired the captive Federal horse ridden by Private Koiner when disabled by that Yankee bullet. The new owner was Private James M. Larew, who in January 1863, at age nineteen, had been transferred to the 1st Virginia from an infantry unit he had served with since his enlistment. Larew was a student before the war, and like Christian Koiner, also named Augusta County as his home.

The strange and unusual end to Private Larew's life came during the cavalry battle which occurred several miles east of Gettysburg on Friday, July 3. This engagement was the result of orders issued to General Stuart by General Lee after his belated arrival on July 2. Stuart was immediately sent off to guard the far left flank of the Confederate army that day. However, on the next morning, his instructions were more offensive in nature; he was told to push forward toward the Union rear and cause a diversion, while infantry units commanded by General Longstreet assaulted the main Federal line on Cemetery Ridge. In that morning advance on July 3, Stuart's deployment was discovered by Northern mounted troops under General David Gregg. The ensuing action could be called a tactical "draw," but it prevented Jeb Stuart from claiming any measurable success in the campaign, and further eroded his now somewhat tainted military record. Again, Sergeant Haden recorded:

> [I]n a short time...the fight became general and raged with fury....
> Mounted fights never lasted long, but there were more men killed and
> wounded in this fight than I ever saw on any field where the fighting was
> done mounted. I shall not attempt to say who got the better of this engage-
> ment, as they seemed to mutually agreed to quit. One party afraid to ad-
> vance, and the other glad of it. The list of casualties in Company E was
> considerable on this occasion. James La[rew] was riding the same horse
> and saddle that Chris. Koiner was killed on at Hanover a few days before,
> and was shot, the ball passing through the same hole in the saddle, and
> through him, just as it did through Koiner. La[rew]'s dying request was
> that no one else would ride that horse or saddle in a fight, which request
> was strictly adhered to. I don't know what became of the horse, but he
> disappeared from the company; was turned over to the quartermaster, I sup-
> pose, as no one wished to ride him.

Haden may have misspelled Larew's name, but the facts of his comrade's death are correct as far as is known. After being wounded, James Larew was captured by the Yankees, and died two days later on July 5, in his "20th year."

Unfortunately, many of the burials on the cavalry battlefield were never chronicled. Perhaps the distances from Gettysburg, or the scattered positioning of the field hospitals, prevented Dr. O'Neal or others from visiting the sites where graves had been dug. In any event, due to these causes, or simply by his unlucky presence in enemy's hands, a transcript of Private Larew's burial place does not now exist.

> That is all, The soft sky bends
> O'er them, lapped in earth away;
> Her benignest influence lends,
> Dews and rains and radiance sends
> Down upon them, night and day.

I BELIEVE JOHN IS MORTALLY WOUNDED

Private John P. Hite,
Co. H, 33rd Virginia Infantry
Walker's (Stonewall) Brigade, Johnson's Division, Ewell's Corps

The war fought for Southern Independence proved to be anything but a positive experience for the family of Rebecca and Daniel Hite of Page County, Virginia. Not only was independence not forthcoming, but three of their four sons, (out of eight children), died while serving with Company H of the 33rd Regiment. Lieutenant William Hite succumbed to disease in 1861; John Hite did not survive Gettysburg; and Private David Hite was killed at Winchester in September 1864. John, at 22, was the youngest to enlist.

At Gettysburg, the Stonewall Brigade was most heavily engaged on July 3. Their tactical disposition was roughly on the right flank of General Edward Johnson's Division, when it attempted to dislodge the Federals from a fortified ridgeline running south, off Culp's Hill and down to Spangler's Spring. The 33rd Virginia of General James A. Walker's Brigade lost 55 men throughout the battle; Company H went into combat with 36, but its casualties were high—4 killed, 17 wounded, of which three were mortal. John Hite was one of the latter.

A member of Hite's company, George Buswell, kept a diary during the campaign. On a page designated for July 2, he made a notation that the brigade went into line of battle at midnight. On the next day, the third of the month, he added these words:

> Slept a little this morning before light. The 33rd Regt. opened the fight at this point before daylight & sunrise, (3:30). When we had fired all our ammunition, we were relieved by the 4th Regt. We had hard fighting here nearly all day, in which our Brigade suffered severely.... We failed to carry the works in front of us. We fell back after midnight, were not followed by the Yankees.

On July 12, ten days following that engagement, Captain Michael Shuler of Company H notified a friend of Daniel Hite's family that, when last seen on July 3, John's condition had not been good, saying, "To be candid, I believe John is mortally wounded." The captain of course, had no way to know that John was already gone. He had died eight days earlier in a Confederate field hospital. But Captain Shuler had other facts; he pointed out that Private Hite "was wounded early in the day. The ball entered his right shoulder and ranged down towards his left side.... In the evening he appeared much more relieved.... [His brother] David remained with him...."

One of John Hite's brother's, who was not a member of the 33rd but was present at Gettysburg, was Isaac M. Hite, a 27-year-old private and former artilleryman assigned to the headquarter's guard of the Army of Northern Virginia. Isaac sent a first letter home from Hagerstown, Maryland, on July 13. In it he says, "Is it so? yes, tis so, John is dead." Further on, Isaac explained, it was John's request, and David's desire, that David stay behind to wait on John and "to have him as neatly buried as he could in the enemy's Country." (David Hite remained behind a prisoner, but survived the war; he was the only one of Rebecca and Daniel's soldier sons to come home alive.)

Isaac's letter gave more details to the family, and added personal sentiments for his lost brother:

> He was shot—the ball entered the right side just below the armpit, passed through near the heart to the left side, ranging down and to the front, and stopped just before Coming through. Shortly after[,] his left side turned black which shows that the ball lodged just under the skin.... He was conscious of his situation, and prayed for death that he might be relieved of his suffering....
>
> But alas he is gone! He was the second son and brother to be called from this world of trouble to eternity.... While his body lies beneath the enemies soil at Gettysburg, we hope his spirit has passed to a better world where no enemy can hurt him again.

Five days later, Isaac wrote from Bunker Hill, Virginia, and told his brother and sister that John was shot on the morning of the third, "before firing his gun," and that he knew as soon as the bullet hit him that he was killed. John also described his own wound, saying it felt as if "their were a dozen balls in his body." Later that evening, Isaac was told by a fellow Virginian that John "could scarcely talk above a whisper," and declared he could not live until morning.

In viewing this event, using all of the surviving sources, it is possible to reconstruct the sequence of occurrences from John Hite's wounding to his burial and reinterrment. In the first place, following Hite's injury, several soldiers of Company H carried him off the Culp's Hill battlefield to a safe area near an ambulance collecting point. There John waited until he could be picked up and conveyed to a field hospital. In the process of removing him, and while still under severe enemy rifle fire, Hite told his companions to "lay him down, and save themselves," for he already believed death was inevitable. This plea was repeated several times, said an eyewitness, but the men eventually got Hite out from under the deadly missiles.

Walker's Brigade hospital was the ultimate destination, and it was already established on the Hunterstown Road, three miles northeast of Culp's Hill. This facility was situated on the farm of Charlotte and Henry Picking, and became the primary medical station for "Stonewall's" old command. The farmstead consisted of a wood and brick house, a barn and other outbuildings, and a brick schoolhouse which sat just southwest of the barn. Henry and Charlotte were kindly remembered by one Confederate officer as being very compassionate to the Southerners who occupied their premises for several weeks. Besides David Hite, there were several other soldier-nurses present at Picking's, and at least one surgeon, possibly a Dr. Roger B. Taney.

Sadly for John Hite, it appears he exhaled his last breaths early on July 4. His brother David gave him a decent burial, and properly marked the gravesite. This is certain, for John's headboard was visible and recorded as such in late 1863, also in October 1864, again in May 1866, and even as late as 1872. The brigade cemetery was placed on high ground directly across the Hunterstown Road from the little schoolhouse. That spot is clearly visible today, and in fact, as this is written, there is a "for sale" sign posted on the little historic crest. So it is likely that a modern house will be built soon, on the site, blighting forever that "hallowed ground."

At any rate, when John Hite arrived, barely alive, at the Picking's farm, he would not have been alone in his agony, for scores of the brigade's wounded were there, as the unit's rolls tallied over 200 injured in the battle. Finally, in death, Hite and 13 other Virginians were carried to the hospital cemetery. There were probably more interred in those days, but when Dr. John O'Neal went around the battlefield and various hospitals compiling his burial lists, that was the number of marked graves he discovered on the farm grounds. O'Neal's exact record states that the 15 men were buried at "Pickings Place in [a] field, along fence opposite the schoolhouse."

Much later, in 1872, when Dr. Rufus Weaver began his exhumations, he visited the site, dug up and placed the remains of John Hite and the 14 others in "Box I-170," for the trip to Hollywood Cemetery in Richmond. He cited them as coming from "Johnson's Div. Hospital on Mr. J. H. [sic] Picking's place about two and half miles N. E. of Gettysburg—not far from the school house and near Hunterstown road."

Weaver made one other entry in his notebook at this site. The memorandum concerned a unique discovery with the skeletal remains in the grave of John Hite. It was a "Front (?) Gold plate and teeth in upper Jaw." In the postwar years, had anyone from John's family attempted to claim his body, this information would have made it possible to positively identify the remains. As it turned out, however, no such endeavor seems to have been undertaken, even though Page County, Virginia, is not an especially long distance from Adams County in Pennsylvania.

Therefore, all that is left of John Hite lies in Richmond, together with the 14 comrades he died with, and surrounded by thousands of others in rotted boxes, who are the Confederate dead of Gettysburg.

> All is gone for them. They gave
> All for naught. It was their way
> Where they loved. They died to save
> What was lost. The fight was brave.
> That is all; and here are they.

John Hite and others of the old Stonewall Brigade were buried on this little knoll in front of the Picking farm schoolhouse. (sch)

IT IS NOT LIKELY THAT WE SHALL MEET AGAIN

Captain William H. Murray,
Co. A, 1st Maryland Battalion
Steuart's Brigade, Johnson's Division, Ewell's Corps

In the city of Baltimore there is a cemetery called Loudon Park, and within that huge burial ground is a section known as "Confederate Hill." "Confederate Hill" is filled with many hundreds of graves of Southern soldiers and veterans who died during and after the Civil War. (There are less than ten known who fell at Gettysburg). Sitting in the midst of the scores of little stones that mark the final resting places of those men, are two larger memorials. The first is a monument built to honor the memory of all the Confederates who lie in the cemetery. It was dedicated in 1870 and is surmounted by a white marble statue of a standing Southern soldier. Just across from this impressive marker is another memorial erected in 1874. It is 11 feet high, incorporating a "broken column" motif of Italian marble, topped by a cluster of laurel leaves. On one of its sides is sculpted the state seal of Maryland, with a presentation from members of the 1st Maryland, and below that seal another inscription reads:

Capt. Wm. H. Murray.

BORN at West River, Md. April 30, 1839.

KILLED at Gettysburg, Pa. July 3, 1863.

This monument indicates that Captain Murray is buried near its location. But the captain is not there. The memorial is just that—it stands in memory of William Murray and the men he commanded. He is interred elsewhere, and we shall learn where in a moment. But first, a little of his story.

From the beginning to the very end of the war, Maryland was a state of divided loyalties. In June 1861, sympathizers of the Confederacy began to organize the 1st Maryland Infantry Regiment. Among its early members was William Henry Murray who led Company H. When, after a year of hard and faithful service, the unit was disbanded, many of the original officers and enlisted men sought to form a new regiment to be called the 2nd Maryland. Unable to entice enough men into the ranks to fill the quota of a full regiment, (about 1,040 in all), a battalion of six companies was formed instead. This new organization was named the 1st Maryland Battalion, though oddly, it is often referred to in writings as the 2nd Maryland Battalion.

One of the first men to enlist a company in the 1st Battalion was William Murray, and his new unit was designated with the letter "A." Fellow soldier George W. Booth became proud of his captain during the early months of service, and called that officer "the noble Murray," saying he was a "paladin of gentle graces, with irreproachable courage and [had the] ability to command men." Another comrade fondly remembered Murray as the "beau ideal of a soldier, straight as an arrow, brave as a lion, chivalrous as any knight of old, gentle as a woman, with the laughing blue eyes and the yellow hair of the Saxton,..."

During the Battle of Gettysburg, the battalion, as part of General George H. Steuart's Brigade, held the left of Johnson's Division and participated in the fighting south of Culp's Hill, on both the evening of July 2, and the morning of the third. For a unit smaller than the normal regiment, the 1st Maryland still carried into action a respectable number of infantrymen, about 400. But it lost nearly half of this compliment during two hard days of combat. And Captain Murray gave up his own life on July 3.

In the early morning hours of that day, the Confederate attack was resumed from the evening before, with General Edward Johnson's Division continuing its assaults on reinforced Northern troops who held strong positions behind barricades erected along the ridge line between Culp's Hill and Spangler's Spring. Many of the men of Steuart's Brigade were not very receptive to these renewed orders, and considered the plan to take the Yankee works impossible to accomplish. They had already seen and tested the dispositions of the enemy, and as one officer noted, "it was nothing less than murder to send men into that slaughter pen." William Murray, as senior captain, very likely agreed, however the directive had to be followed. But in realizing the difficulty of the task facing his men, Captain Murray took a few minutes prior to the advance to shake the hand of every soldier in his company, saying to them, "Good-bye, it is not likely that we shall meet again."

Soon, General Steuart ordered bayonets fixed, and gave the command, "Attention! Forward, double-quick! March!" The line surged toward the Union breastworks 200 yards away across an open field. Captain Murray, sword upraised, urged his men onward, calling out: "Use your bayonets, boys; don't fire." Then a deadly crossfire erupted into the Marylanders at 100 yards, toppling Confederates at every step. Murray, still standing, continued to charge with Company A, moving closer and closer to the enemy's earthworks. But William Murray's luck soon ran out. He received a death wound in the neck when very near to the Yankee entrenchments, and his brother, Private Alexander Murray, rushed to catch his dying body. Then almost immediately, Alexander was knocked unconscious by the explosive concussion of an artillery shell. Promptly, a second brother, Lieutenant Clapham Murray, stepped up and assumed command of the company. A Marylander named Randolph McKim, said of that moment: "That brave officer and noble gentleman, Captain Murray, fell dead. Friends dropped all around me, and lay writhing on the ground.... It was more than men could endure, and reluctantly they commenced falling back."

The charge had been unsuccessful, but close fighting continued until noon. During those hours, some battalion members lay under the dangerous fire of friend and foe alike. Private James W. Thomas of Company A was one of these trapped men:

> While lying on the battlefield, I was grieved to see poor Bill Murray stretched out stiff and cold. Oh! how I felt. I liked him, and he was a fine soldier, a fine Captain. He used to look forward with such pride and joy to an entrance into Baltimore, and to think his life was thrown away. [H]ad the left

been properly conducted and supported, the loss might have been small, and there was a chance of [us] gaining the advantage which would have won the battle. But all was disordered, the men slaughtered.

An ordnance officer of Longstreet's Corps, Captain F. M. Colston, recalled how deadly this action was to Murray's company. He had visited with these Marylanders on July 1, and later he was glad he did:

> Most of my friends were in Company A, Capt. William H. Murray, and when I left them I said good-bye to many of them forever, for two days afterward they charged on Culp's Hill, and lost sixty-seven out of ninety-eight in that company, the gallant Billy Murray being killed at their head—only twenty-four years old.

When the battle ended, the Federal army retained control of the entire area around Culp's Hill. For that reason, almost all of the Confederate dead were interred as unknowns in mass graves, some containing between 40 and 100

Capt. Murray led his company straight toward the Yankee line.

bodies each. Somehow Captain Murray's corpse escaped this dismal fate. His corpse must have been recovered by the men of his company and given a proper burial. These soldiers, the comrades he loved like brothers, returned that affection with this dangerous, worthy and important gesture.

Within several weeks of the battle, the kindness of Murray's men paid off. William Murray's half-sister Elizabeth, and a family servant, boarded a wagon and made the difficult journey from southern Anne Arundel County to Gettysburg. There, they found William's grave, and returned its contents to the family plot in West River, Maryland.

So the story has reached its conclusion. It is still not known why Captain Murray's memorial lies so far from his grave in West River. Perhaps his surviving comrades in Baltimore simply needed and wanted a tangible remembrance close at hand. For them it would be a physical tribute towering among their dead, a daily reminder of how they had once known real greatness, and true nobility.

Capt. Murray was honored in Baltimore with this monument.

105

THE MOST APPALLING SCENE

Lieutenant Daniel A. Featherston,
Co. F, 11th Mississippi Infantry
Davis' Brigade, Heth's Division, Hill's Corps

There appears to be no right way to categorize the death of a soldier in battle. Trying to do so seems unfair to the humans thus affected. It might be because every death in combat usually happens to a younger and vibrant man, and is not an easy thing to bear. And, too, it does not seem quite right to differentiate between the many types of deaths, as all do the same harm. To eyewitnesses of these morbid events, there is normally an automatic and instinctive response of shock or amazement when someone dies violently. This can hardly be helped. It is especially true if the person is not a stranger to the onlooker, and if the death is particularly gruesome. Usually if they live long enough, infantrymen in wartime see every guise taken by the "Grim Reaper." And it follows that sometimes soldiers cannot help making distinctions when a comrade meets a singularly grisly fate, almost as if by describing the event it will help to dull its horror. The following story of a Mississippi lieutenant is a good example of this.

Daniel Featherston of Macon, was 25 and a mechanic when he joined a unit from Noxubee County on April 25, 1861. He must have been readily noticed in his company, for someone described him "as a large man—[who] would have weighed perhaps two hundred pounds." For a year Featherston was a private. He was then promoted to corporal, and five months later he was commissioned a junior 2nd lieutenant. Shortly thereafter, he was made a 2nd lieutenant, a position he held during the campaign into Pennsylvania.

Until Gettysburg, and even through the first two days of that engagement, Daniel Featherston's fortunes had been lucky. His military record does not indicate any injuries or bouts with sickness for the two years and nearly three months following his enlistment. And during that span of time his regiment had passed through at least seven major actions.

This remarkable pace all changed on the early afternoon of July 3, as the men of the 11th Mississippi waited behind a low ridge a mile or so southwest of Gettysburg. Over and around them, more than 200 cannon dueled furiously, throwing shot and shell at each other for nearly two hours. One of the Mississippians commented almost poetically on that deafening storm of projectiles: "Peal on peal, in one continuous roar, belched forth the dread artillery while the very atmosphere around us, became vocal with the humming of the death-dealing demons that whistled by."

The Confederate army was then preparing for what would forever be known as the "Pickett-Pettigrew Charge," an American historical event that Lt. Featherston would never hear about, write about, or experience. For when that hour arrived, while his companions struggled to keep alive their own futures, Daniel Featherston lay still, his crushed body freed from the trials and tribulations surrounding him. A member of Company A named Baker later recalled the lieutenant's instantaneous transformation from living being to crumpled corpse:

> I...remember one Featherstone [sic] in the Noxubee Rifles. While we were lying down on Seminary Ridge,...just behind our batteries,...and just before we went into the charge on Cemetery Heights, Featherstone was struck by a cannon ball and thrown several feet in the air, his head being split wide open.

Private Andrew Baker was not the only soldier stunned by the sight. First Lieutenant William Peel, an officer in Company C, added a long paragraph about that moment to his personal diary:

> In the hot[t]est of the cannonading I heard a shell strike in the right of the reg't & turning over, as I lay upon my back, I looked just in time to witness the most appal[l]ing scene that perhaps ever greeted the human eye. Lt. Daniel Featherston...was the unfortunate victim.... He was lying on his face, when the shell struck the ground near his head, &, in the ricochet, entered his breast, exploding about the same time & knocking him at least ten feet high, & not less than twenty feet from where he was lying.

How transient is life, how unstable the future, how quickly we pass, how soon we are forgotten.

For death the mighty reaper comes
To rich as well as poor.
Unwelcome guest though he may be,
He comes to every door.

On an 1863 map of the Gettysburg battlefield, the location of Davis' Brigade during the bombardment preceding "Pickett's Charge" is basically about three-quarters of a mile east of a small farm which sits along the Fairfield (also known as the Millerstown or Hagerstown) Road, where it crosses Willoughby's Run. During the Civil War years the land and buildings of this farm were owned by Gettysburg businessman George Arnold, but were rented to John Horting. It appears that the medical staff of Davis' Brigade, including the 11th Mississippi, made use of the little farmstead as a temporary aid or dressing station. It was here that the torn body of Lt. Featherston was carried for an initial interment.

Shortly following the battle, and probably before the end of December, Dr. John O'Neal completed his first catalogue of the Confederate graves in Adams County. In that tabulation are seven Southern soldiers under "John Hortons" name, all lying "near the Garden fence." They were all members of the 2nd, 11th, and 42nd Mississippi regiments, except one attributed to the 55th North Carolina. One of those burials was "Lieut. Fedtferston," of Co. F, 11th Mississippi. Sometime after this, either in October 1864 or May 1866, O'Neal shows "Lieut. Fetherston" and four

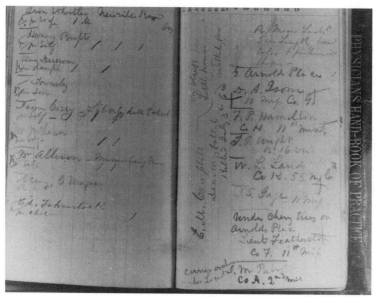

Lt. Featherston's grave was recorded in Dr. O'Neal's handbook, which saved his identity from being lost. (achs)

other graves located at "Arnold's Place—Millerstown road—Under cherry tree," and a notation that reads, "see Mis[s]. list Octo 10-64." From these jottings it is known that Daniel Featherston's body remained at Horting's, or Arnold's, farm until 1872-3, because his remains were shown then being transferred to Hollywood Cemetery in Richmond. In checking copies of Dr. Rufus Weaver's original shipment papers to that cemetery, Featherston's name appears with a group of 38 remains, "whose graves can be identified but not separately. These can be packed in boxes, each box having some marks on it to indicate,...the respective remains in each box. These are buried in separate 'state' lots *and not* promiscuously." Oddly though, Weaver does also mention that in a box marked "A" in one of his exhumations, there were twelve sets of bones, five of which were named. Four of these identified remains were recovered from "Mr Arnolds farm—one mile S. W. of Gettysburg on Hagerstown road—under a walnut tree S. E. corner of Garden." Three of the four were the same men who had previously been found by Dr. O'Neal side by side with Lieutenant Featherston "near the Garden fence."

So Daniel Featherston's name is present on Weaver's register, and he turns up in the official inventory at Hollywood Cemetery as an identified Confederate, removed by Dr. Weaver. He was therefore either part of the 38 remains in 'state' lots, or one of the 12 from under the walnut tree. His final disposition must remain, for now at least, as just another intriguing footnote to the great and bloody Battle of Gettysburg.

USHERED INTO ETERNITY

Sergeant Joseph F. Lynn,
Co. G, 8th Virginia Infantry
Garnett's Brigade, Pickett's Division, Longstreet's Corps

The most interesting part of writing this little book has been the experience of identifying, for the first time in almost 140 years, a few Confederate soldiers whose death stories were described by their contemporaries, but whose names were not provided, or were unknown at the time. Discovering the identities of these up-to-now "lost" men has been a great and pleasing reward. The following is an example of one such discovery.

When a visitor to the Gettysburg battlefield hears or reads about casualties inflicted to Northern or Southern troops in "Longstreet's Assault" of July 3, they almost immediately think of the direct fire of cannons and muskets during the ground attack itself. It is often forgotten that a nearly two hour Confederate bombardment, replied to by at least 90 Federal artillery pieces, preceded the infantry "charge." Both sides suffered the loss of men and horses killed and wounded by thousands of iron projectiles thrown back and forth during that afternoon, between the hours of one and three.

The Virginians of Pickett's Division were no exception. In some companies in the regiments of Generals Kemper, Garnett, and Armistead, actual casualties from the cannonade were quite high, especially since the bombardment was not really considered the "main event."

One unit which took its share of damage from artillery fire was the 8th Virginia, a regiment organized in May 1861 at Leesburg. There were 193 rank and file present at Gettysburg, all commanded by Colonel Norborne Berkeley. How many of Berkeley's soldiers were hit by Yankee shot and shell prior to the attack is unknown, but in summary, the colonel lost 178, including those captured. That is an amazing 92.2% reduction of his force, and it all happened in less than three hours.

One member of the 8th who was present that awful day was 19-year-old Private Randolph A. Shotwell. He remembered two deaths that came suddenly from the sky above, and in 1876 he wrote about them:

> Reclining in front of my company, I was watching the struggles of a wounded artillery horse, when a shell whizzed over my head, and struck behind me. Seeing a peculiar expression upon the countenance of an officer, who was looking back, I also glanced around, and saw a most shocking spectacle. The heavy missile had descended six feet behind me, and *ploughed through* the bodies of Morris and Jackson of my own company. Poor fellows! they were devoted friends, and lay side by side on their blankets: and side by side were ushered into eternity!

According to Shotwell, Privates Albert J. Morris and Benjamin E. Jackson, both of Company D, were killed in the first ten minutes of the cannonade. Their "mangled remains" were immediately carried to the rear.

Norborne Berkeley had a similar story to tell while waiting for the order to advance against Cemetery Ridge. And if possible, his example was even more ghastly than the one just reported. "We were lying behind a slight elevation with our artillery in front," said the colonel, "and when the artillery duel commenced, the enemy soon got our range and one of his shells struck one of the sergeants behind whom I was lying, tearing his head into fragments, and plastering his brains over my hat."

Unlike Shotwell, Colonel Berekely chose not to identify, or did not know or remember the sergeant he saw decapitated. In justice to that soldier, some simple research has made it possible to reveal his name. He was Joseph F. Lynn of Company G, who had enlisted in July 1861 as a private, but was promoted to sergeant on March 1, 1863. Unfortunately, this bit of information is all that can be gleaned from the historical record.

In like fashion, the facts relating to Sergeant Lynn's burial are even more indefinite. If he or Morris or Jackson was interred there along Seminary Ridge, or at the field hospital of Pickett's Division near Bream's Mineral Mills, no record remains to verify it. Correspondingly, neither physician, O'Neal or Weaver, ever appeared to have encountered their graves. Possibly, in the heat and fury of the moment, or in the disastrous aftermath of the charge and retreat, no one took notice of a few missing soldiers. That day, while defeat and confusion reigned for the survivors of Pickett's command, three of their comrades who also died for a common cause and country, were forgotten.

And their bodies, like so many others, were left to the unforgiving ravages of time, and the indifference of nature's hand.

HE WAS A SENSIBLE INTELLIGENT MAN

Captain James M. Kincaid,
Co. G, 52nd North Carolina Infantry
Pettigrew's Brigade, Heth's Division, Hill's Corps

The average size of an infantry brigade in Lee's army during the early stages of the Gettysburg Campaign was probably about 1,500 men. One of the largest going into the campaign was that of General James J. Pettigrew, with a strength of 2,581. Its losses in the three day battle reached 1,450. Had it mustered the standard number above, by the evening of July 3, the brigade would have been wiped out.

Pettigrew's Brigade was in combat both on the first and last day of the battle, and probably all of its casualties were inflicted on those two days. On Friday, July 3, Pettigrew's much reduced regiments participated in what is now known as "Pickett's Charge;" a misnomer for what most military historians call "Longstreet's Assault," named after the general who planned and executed this final Confederate attack against the Union army at Gettysburg.

When the fighting ended that final day, several thousand men were left dead or injured on the fields that separated Seminary Ridge from Cemetery Ridge. One of the mortally wounded was Captain James Kincaid, who lay somewhere in front of a stone wall which ran along a portion of the second named ridge. He had been shot in the left thigh, a dangerous injury which usually required amputation, especially if the artery was cut or the bone was broken.

As soon as it was safely possible, groups of Northern soldiers left their protective positions and went among the Confederates, some to round up prisoners, some to collect souvenirs or trophies, and some to succor the wounded. In the latter group, was a member of the 14th Connecticut Infantry, Sergeant Alexander McNeil. The sergeant happened upon a suffering officer from North Carolina, and administered what aid he could until the overworked ambulance teams could transport the injured man to a U. S. medical facility. That Southerner was likely Captain J. M. Kincaid. In a letter written two weeks after the campaign, McNeil, who did not survive the war, told a friend how he met the North Carolinian:

> At the time that the Rebels made their last desperate charge, our Division came in for their share of fighting. The Rebels came up in fine style, with 3 lines of Battle....
>
> Our Brigade was lying behind some Rails, piled up & a low stone wall & we paid the Rebels back, with *Interest*, for our defeat at Fredericksburg.
>
> I had a long conversation with a Captain of the 52nd. North Carolina Regt. He was severely wounded & we carried him into our lines & laid him down. I gave him coffee to drink twice, while waiting for a stretcher to carry him to the Hospital. He was a sensible Intelligent man. He told me the South had been rough & harsh with the North Carolina troops all through, since the War commenced. He told me that it was because the State of North Carolina did not *Secede* quite soon enough to suit some of the other Slave States. He told me, too, that the State of South Carolina ought to be sunk. That, he said, was where the trouble started.

The sentiments expressed by Captain Kincaid were not unusual. The fact is, large numbers of Southerners were not in favor of secession. This belief was prevalent in various areas of the Confederacy, and was especially true in some counties of North Carolina. These ideas were expressed by many prisoners interviewed at Gettysburg. However, once the war began, most men like

Kincaid stood with their state in the quest for independence, and fought bravely to the end.

Once ambulances were freed up from carrying Union casualties to the rear, Captain Kincaid and his comrades were picked up and taken to the field hospital of the Second Army Corps on the Jacob Schwartz farm, three miles southward, which was situated between two streams, Rock Creek and White Run. When Camp Letterman U. S. General Hospital opened on the York Turnpike about the middle of July, many wounded Confederates were transferred there. Kincaid was one of these men. Government records indicate that he was a patient at the new camp until his death on August 27, 1863. The staff at Letterman kept an accurate cemetery burial roster, and Captain Kincaid's name is among the bodies interred there. He was in Grave # 14, in Row 6, but he is listed as a member of the 57th North Carolina, rather than the 52nd regiment. Therefore, on the list of identified North Carolina remains removed from Gettysburg by the Wake County Ladies' Memorial Association in the fall of 1871, the name of "C. C. Kincaid, Co. G, 57th North Carolina" appears. Since "C. C. Kincaid" was not a member of the 57th and was not killed at Gettysburg, it is probable that the misidentification occurred simply because the name and regimental number on Kincaid's grave marker became weathered and harder to read as the years passed.

Captain Kincaid was only 23 when he died in one of the white canvas hospital tents at Camp Letterman. He had enlisted in Lincoln County, a county with a large Unionist population, in the spring of 1862. Whatever sentiments he had toward the war, there is no denying that from his entrance into the army and up through July 3, 1863, James Kincaid had done his full duty to the Confederate States of America.

On that hellish mile-long journey, from one ridge to another, the captain was at his post. He fell with his face toward the enemies of his homeland, and then only a few terrible feet from his goal.

No man could ask for a more honorable epitaph.

I SAW HIS SPIRIT HAD FLED

Captain William R. Bissell,
Co. A, 8th Virginia Infantry
Garnett's Brigade, Pickett's Division, Longstreet's Corps

The dreaded letter arrived in Bel-Air, in northern Virginia, on July 11, 1863. It was addressed to Margaret Bissell, and on one of its pages she read the ominous words her husband William had written while lying wounded in a U. S. hospital near Gettysburg, Pennsylvania. The announcement that he was injured, but *not very dangerously*, took away some of the initial shock and fear she felt upon opening the envelope.

Unfortunately, Captain Bissell had not told Margaret the whole truth. For in fact, the situation in Gettysburg was much more grave than he had written. On July 3, in his 13th battle, Bissell had led Company A, among more than 11,000 other Confederate soldiers, across nearly a mile of open ground toward a Federal battle line on Cemetery Ridge. In the process, the captain first had been stunned by the explosion of a shell. This calamity was followed by a bullet which struck the fleshy part of one of his legs, just above the knee; and finally, two balls hit the top of the left arm near the shoulder.

For 48 hours Captain Bissell lay on the ground where he fell, most of the time spent in the rain with no shelter. Eventually Union personnel found him, and he was removed to the field hospital of the 2nd Division, Second Corps, where he was placed on a rubber blanket in a small fly tent with four other men.

Immediately upon receipt of this bad news, Margaret Bissell went into action. After hurried preparations, she began the slow trip to Gettysburg with Lizzie, one of her daughters, and Mr. Burns Duval, a hired man. Early on July 14, the trio arrived in Baltimore, where the necessary papers were obtained. These documents gave Margaret an "official" position with the U. S. Christian Commission so she could travel freely. In the city she was met by Dr. Hall Richardson, and another physician named Lee. Then at eight the next morning the five boarded a train for the battlefield. Arriving at midnight the group procured lodging and an early breakfast. Afterward, Lizzie, Margaret, and Dr. Richardson went afield to locate Captain Bissell, whom they were told was at the Army of the Potomac's Eleventh Corps Hospital.

After a long walk and a fruitless search, the tired, but resolute party headed further south to the Second Corps' site. In Margaret's words, they "trudg[ed] through the mud and beneath a scorching sun, making [their] way among dead horses, army wagons and soldiers articles of every description." By late afternoon all were exhausted, but still not at their goal, so were forced to stop for rest at a farmhouse. After a while, the doctor went on alone. When he returned he brought good news; the captain had been found lying amidst several thousand wounded at the hospital of the Second Corps.

When Margaret Bissell first saw her husband she removed her bonnet and went to him. She explained: "I then knelt by his side and kissed him, he called Lizzie to kiss him and remarked that I was looking very well." The family was instructed by Dr. Richardson that although William looked well, unless the arm came off he would die. Margaret remembered that the bones "were all shattered, and his arm and side were very much swollen, [with] every indication of erysipelas," an infectious skin disease. Lizzie meanwhile, thought that her father should have a private tent. So, determined to acquire this luxury for the captain, Lizzie and Margaret went directly to hospital headquarters.

For the wife and daughter of a "Rebel," they were kindly received, but a surgeon declared that no tents were available. But much to their relief, two Union soldiers were standing nearby and overheard the request. They offered to help, and soon canvas was found, and Mrs. Bissell said the men went to work "as willingly as if I had been an old acquaintance." When the tent was ready, Margaret made up a bed and undertook to clean William's wounds with wine, and give his entire body an alcohol bath. When this task was completed, the captain was dressed in new underclothes and given beef soup, wine, and other delicacies.

For a while during this pleasant interlude, Captain Bissell visited with his wife and daughter, telling them in detail of his military experiences before and during the recent fight. But the inevitable could not be postponed. The captain, for the third time in thirteen days, was again transferred to a stretcher, but this time he was carried to an operating table, where his arm was amputated at the shoulder by Surgeon C. S. Wood, 66th New York. The arm was removed on Thursday morning, July 16. Had there been a clock nearby, its face would have placed the time about eleven o'clock.

According to Dr. Richardson, the procedure went well and William bore it better than expected. For the next several hours the captain drifted in and out of sleep, and was often awakened and asked questions by the three persons near his bed. William always replied, but then would fall back into sleep. Once during those trying hours, Bissell remarked that he was prepared to die, saying he felt perfectly comfortable about it. This vigil was kept up until almost midnight, when at that moment, Margaret noticed William "opened wide his eyes and mouth and I saw his spirit had fled."

The next day a coffin was purchased, and the captain's body was cleaned and prepared for burial by Margaret herself, after which the corpse was driven to Evergreen Cemetery near Gettysburg. When admission was denied there, the dedicated doctors Lee and Richardson procured a place in the "Presbyterian Church Yard" which was on High Street across from the Catholic Church. By seven p.m. the grave was dug, the services said, and a headboard placed over the spot, all completed by the two physicians, Mr. Duval, and five Union soldiers. By eight the next morning everyone connected to Captain Bissell was enroute back to Baltimore.

Meanwhile, as Margaret's train rolled southward, the captain's second daughter, Fannie, was on a northbound train heading to Gettysburg to seek out her wounded father. Fannie arrived at three a.m. on the 17th, and at daylight began to hunt for William, going in a ten mile radius around the battlefield until she too collapsed from the fatigue of the arduous search. Fortunately, a passing army wagon filled with wounded soldiers came across Fannie and carried her back to Gettysburg. With no word of her father, she finally boarded a train for Baltimore, arriving at one a.m. on Monday morning.

By ten p.m., Fannie was home, according to Margaret, "a changed girl, the sufferings she has gone through [was] almost more than she will be able to bear." In summarizing her own difficult journey, Margaret pronounced that the Federal surgeons had attended [William] very faithfully, and finished by saying:

> We have to be thankful for many kindnesses during our stay in Gettysburg as we received every attention that it was possible for men to bestow. There was no difference shown on account of Mr. Bissell's politics and he was kept in the Union camp and not sent to the Rebel.

Captain Bissell's grave at the old Presbyterian cemetery was still clearly marked in May 1866, but by then he had been joined by a companion, Corporal John R. Young, of Co. G, 3rd North Carolina. And when most of the Confederate remains were removed to the South between 1870-73, the captain's bones were boxed and shipped to Hollywood Cemetery, where they remain to this day.

As a last thought, there is probably little doubt that all are curious to know if William's grave was ever visited by his beloved Margaret. Yet, since the Richmond site is a collective burial, she could not have been sure exactly where he lay. However, that aside, what would have been her thoughts, as she paused, standing on the grass that covered her husband's earthy tomb? And would it have mattered, really, as her warm tears touched the ground, under which her hopes and dreams, and love, were buried forever.

Many of Capt. Bissell's fellow wounded lay in this barn
at the U.S. Second Corps Hospital. (gac)

I AM WITH YOU

Private William H. McCulloch,
Co. H, 14th Tennessee Infantry
Archer's Brigade, Heth's Division, Hill's Corps

To experience moments of sheer terror is quite rare in our society today. But there will always be the adventurous among us who continually search for the ultimate challenge, where the chance of death is near and present, and where fear is actually enjoyed for the adrenalin rush it produces. These posed experiences are different from the dread felt before and during a battle. To see death surrounding you, searching for you, in its various and sundry faces, ugly with possibilities, becomes a more personal terror.

Death's normal battlefield guise back then was in the form of lifeless missiles made of metal—iron and lead usually—and when they came around these voices of death hissed and screamed and thundered, and their exploding fingers reached out and tore human skin and bone into meaningless and insignificant debris. As a soldier once noted, encountering this style of excitement could be something else entirely.

Yet, through such menace, to still possess the courage to stand up and keep going forward is surely the crux of the matter. And curiously, through time, human nature often responded as indifferently to the terrors of war, as did Billy McCulloch on July 3, 1863.

In every way, William McCulloch was one of the best of his generation. Born in 1842, and reared in Clarksville, Tennessee, his youth was spent in the usual enjoyments of work, school and college, right up until his enlistment into Captain Frank Beaumont's company of the 14th Tennessee in 1861. One officer of that regiment, Captain Junius Kimble, described McCulloch as "one whose courage, fidelity to duty, and loyalty to the cause was not surpassed by any Confederate Soldier." Furthermore, said Kimble, "he was eminently a christian, patient, gentle, firm, and as lovable as a woman... [and] one of the most consistent young men, in all his acts and career as a soldier I ever knew. His moral courage, if possible, was superior to his physical."

With attributes like these, there is little doubt that Private McCulloch would always be where he was suppose to be, and without being told. That premise was proven in the mid-afternoon of July 3, as Archer's Brigade surged toward the crest of the Union fortifications at Gettysburg amidst a hailstorm of deadly projectiles, whose only purpose was to seek out and destroy living beings. In that moment, Billy McCulloch revealed the highest proof of his heroic character; he shed his life's blood at the very foot of Cemetery Ridge.

Captain Kimble remembered it all. When two-thirds of the way across the open fields, a crushing fire caused gap after gap to appear in the Southern ranks. Closing these spaces, which men had so recently filled, narrowed General Archer's regimental fronts to the few staunch Tennesseans and Alabamians resigned to the doleful task before them. When only one hundred feet remained to reach the enemy wall, Kimble spied next to him one of his own men, the bravest and best of Company A, Theodore Hartman. Hartman as always, Kimble said, was "calm and fearless," and had stepped up to his captain's right side and declared the two should "stay together." And this they agreed, "mid the roar of cannons and the rattle of musketry." Before another thirty feet had been gained, William McCulloch moved up to Kimble's left side, "shoulder to shoulder," and Captain Kimble spoke up saying, "Billy, stay with us." To that request came the immediate reply: "I am with you."

"But hardly had his courageous response passed from his lips," said Kimble, "when a deadly minnie pierced his brain, and he fell with his face to the foe and died without a struggle."

After it was over, and the Confederates were forced to retreat, the wounded and the dead were all that remained to mark the passage of Archer's Brigade, and the other brave little bands who had attempted the impossible. The burials on this part of the field were completed quickly and methodically by the victors. In the end, though, the youthful scions of Tennessee and Alabama, Virginia, Mississippi and North Carolina, had crowned those deadly heights with valor, but bitter defeat was their only reward, and rough, unmarked graves their eternal memorial.

> Festering bone and rotting limb,
> In dire confusion tossed.

It is recorded that William's father later visited the battlefield and used all the resources in his power in trying to find the remains of his precious son. But his efforts were in vain, and he "turned his steps homeward without results."

"Hence today," contemplated Captain Kimble, "[Billy's] ashes rest in peace on the field of his glory,...but the soil which covers his dust is a hundredfold richer by reason of his blood."

I HAVE YOU ON MY MIND

Lieutenant Wesley L. Battle,
Co. D, 37th North Carolina Infantry
Lane's Brigade, Pender's Division, Hill's Corps

This is the kind of tale from which myths are made. It illustrates the good in the human spirit, which, through similar stories of decency and kindness, help to blunt the cruelty and chaos of war. Thankfully, for the good of all, the American Civil War is replete with thousands of these examples. Such accounts are usually very much alike, and similar to the one that follows. It concerns a Confederate lieutenant and a Union private, whose lives, for a brief moment, came together on the field at Gettysburg.

When General James Lane's Brigade marched toward Cemetery Ridge on the afternoon of July 3, it occupied a position of support for the entire left wing of Longstreet's assault. This placed Lane's five North Carolina regiments in rear and on the north side of the attacking force. After crossing the open plain over William Bliss' farm fields, the brigade finally came up toward the enemy held ridge, and closed in on the stone wall held by troops of the Union's Second Corps. There a "murderous artillery and infantry fire" sliced through the Confederate ranks, and General Lane saw his left flank become "very much exposed," when a column of Federals was thrown forward and enfiladed his whole line. One of the Southern soldiers shot down here was 19-year-old Lieutenant Wesley Battle who was hit in the left arm.

Within minutes the attack failed and was essentially over. The men who were not killed, wounded, or captured, hastily returned to the safety of Seminary Ridge. To cover this retreat, a few Confederate units not involved in the main assault pushed ahead from a sunken road on General Lane's left and began to skirmish with U. S. forces in their front. A counter move by the Northern army consisted partly of a portion of General Henry Baxter's Brigade sent to neutralize these skirmishers.

One of Baxter's regiments was the 12th Massachusetts, and a member in the ranks that day was Private Kenneth Hickey of Company E, a 28-year-old bootmaker originally from Weymouth. When the threat had ended, Hickey, like many others, went to the aid of Rebel soldiers who were lying injured and helpless on those bloodstained fields. This is how Lieutenant Battle and Private Hickey must have met. The letter tells the rest:

Lt. Battle was aided on the battlefield by an enemy soldier.

April 16th

Friend Battles

I have been thinking about writing to you for a long time and I have just made out to do it. You may think I have forgot you, but not so, for I have thought of you often. I hope to find you well, but when I left you at Gettysburg you was far from being well. You don't know yet who I be, but I [will] tell you. Do you

118

ever think of the soldier who took care of you at the time you was laying wounded on the field at Gettysburg. Do you recollect the knife you gave me, and you wanted to give me your pistol, and I hid it in your bag, and told you to keep it, for you said you wanted to if you could, for it was given to you. I got home safe but my health is not very good, but you told me to write to you if I got out of it and I have and I hope you have not forgotten me. You told me of your father and mother and a brother that was killed at South Mountain, and I hope to hear from you as soon as you please, for I have you on my mind a great part of the time.

> I remain truly,
> Kenneth Hickey
> % Braintree Mass

This letter never reached the young officer, because he lived only 50 days after meeting Hickey. Wesley Battle, like most of the wounded survivors of "Pickett's Charge," was probably taken to the Federal's Second Corps field hospital for initial treatment, which included the amputation of his arm. When that facility closed at the end of July, all seriously injured patients, including the "Rebels" held there, were moved to Camp Letterman U. S. General Hospital on the York Road east of Gettysburg. Lieutenant Battle died on August 22, and was buried, according to Dr. John O'Neal, in the camp cemetery, Row 5, Grave # 32. In 1866, when Dr. O'Neal began compiling another register of the Confederate dead, Battle's name was not added. And in 1871, when 137 North Carolinians were exhumed by the Wake County Ladies' Memorial Association, he was not one of those removed. Correspondingly, when 3,320 Southern remains were taken from the ground between 1872 and 1873, and shipped to Richmond for permanent reinterrment, Wesley Battle was again absent from those transferred. His grave at Gettysburg was either obliterated between 1863 and 1866, which would have been an unusual occurrence at Camp Letterman, or, his body was recovered by the family, and is now resting in North Carolina.

The latter possibility would be the best to hope for. Private Hickey would certainly have agreed.

THE SECRET BURIAL

Corporal Columbus M. Cook,
Co. D, 11th Mississippi Infantry
Davis' Brigade, Heth's Division, Hill's Corps

There are people today who can tell you which regiments suffered the greatest percentage of losses in the Battle of Gettysburg. If questioned, their analysis will always include, on the Confederate side at least, the 11th Mississippi. For example, in one instance alone, and in less than an hour of fighting, the 11th lost 89 percent of its men. This took place during the short duration of the "Pickett-Pettigrew Attack" on the afternoon of July 3. One of the casualties on that day is the subject of this narrative, Corporal Columbus M. Cook.

Born on November 28, 1840, near Coffadeliah in eastern Neshoba County, Columbus Cook was one of six brothers who went off to war for Mississippi and the Confederate States of America during the years 1861-62; all eventually became members of the same unit, Company D, 11th Mississippi. The six young men were the sons of Michael and Winaford Evans Cook, planters and merchants, whose family consisted of thirteen children. Columbus enlisted on March 1, 1862, and served, apparently uninjured, through the major battles of Seven Pines, Gaines's Mill, Malvern Hill, Second Manassas, South Mountain, and Sharpsburg. This streak of good fortune, held through so many close encounters with death, came to a bloody end in Pennsylvania during the midsummer of 1863.

Approximately a dozen or so years ago, the great-great grandson of Michael Cook, Mr. Steven H. Stubbs, began to compile his family history as a gift to his children. In the process, he also included an interesting and detailed section on the 11th Mississippi regiment during the Civil War. One of his findings was an unusual account concerning the burial of Corporal Columbus Cook. And as it was his research which uncovered the fascinating details, Mr. Stubbs completes the sad tale:

About midafternoon on the 3rd of July 1863, Corporal Columbus Martin Cook was killed during the charge on the Federal lines on Cemetery Hill. Private Jacob Harrison Cook was captured that same day, probably around the 'high-water' line near the wall at the Brian barn or during the retreat of the Eleventh down from Cemetery Ridge. During the night after the great battle, Private William Buford Cook went back onto the battlefield to search for the body of his fallen brother. After finding his brother, Columbus Martin Cook, William Cook realized that, because of the number of Confederate dead upon the field, a proper burial was an impossibility. With his bayonet and his hands, he scooped out a grave and buried his brother on the field of battle at the place where he fell. For almost the next sixty-five years, William Buford Cook never revealed a word to anyone about this occurrence. On the 2nd of July 1928, when William Buford Cook was walking on the battlefield at Vicksburg, Mississippi, for the first and only time, he revealed to his son, William Henry Cook, a Justice on the Mississippi Supreme Court, the story of the burial of his brother, Corporal Columbus Martin Cook. The next day, the 3rd of July 1928, exactly sixty-five years to the day after the great battle and the burial of his brother in an unmarked grave along the route of the Pickett/Pettigrew charge, William Buford Cook lay down to rest, perhaps with a great burden lifted, and within an hour, had passed away—the last survivor of the fighting Cook brothers of Company D, Eleventh Infantry Regiment of Mississippi Volunteers.

I FELL AT MY POST

Private Thomas L. Guerry,
Co. B, Sumter Georgia Artillery
Lane's Battalion, Anderson's Division, Hill's Corps

At the very southern end of Seminary Ridge, and on the northern edge of Pitzer Woods, is a cast iron tablet which marks the general locality held by Captain George M. Patterson's Company B, "Sumter Artillery," during the action of July 2, 1863. There, approximately 124 Georgians and six guns of Patterson's company stood and fought for several hours trying to suppress enemy artillery during General Longstreet's late afternoon assault against the Union left flank. The battery had been dispatched to that area by Major John Lane in order to support General Wilcox's infantry brigade. According to Captain Patterson, the second was the only day of the battle that his battery saw action. The captain's two 12-pounder Napoleon's and four 12-pounder howitzers opened on the Yankees probably before four o'clock, and by evening Company B had suffered a loss of one man killed and eight wounded, although another source claims the casualties were two dead and five injured.

An artilleryman of Patterson's company who most certainly died as a result of combat at Gettysburg, (although the exact day of his death is not clear), was Private Thomas Legrande Guerry. Moreover, Guerry did not perish immediately on the battlefield, but apparently expired the following day, in, or enroute to, a Confederate field hospital. This information comes from a soldier in Company A, of Lane's "Sumter Battalion," named Felix R. Galloway.

According to Galloway's recollections, which seem to contradict Captain Patterson, after spending several hours the following day providing artillery support to Southern troops near the David McMillan farm prior to and during the "Pickett-Pettigrew Charge," Company A was sent on the evening of July 3 to another location back of Seminary Ridge to rest and resupply. At this point, Private Galloway's narrative supplies information as to the whereabouts and disposition of Thomas Guerry himself. On the march to the rear, Galloway and a companion had stopped for water on "the Sharpsburg road," which forced them to quicken their pace to catch up with the battery:

> We then hurried forward and found that our company had halted at the hospital camp to inquire concerning our wounded comrades. As I came up Dr. William H. Green, once a member of Company A, said to me: "You see that pile of hands, feet, arms, fingers, ears, toes, and legs, about four bushels, over there? John Tyson's leg and [Thomas Guerry's] arm are in it. We did the best we could for them and sent them further to the rear for safety."

In his version of events, Galloway ended the description of the hospital visit by saying: "They both died that night."

The place Dr. Green alluded to, where Tyson and Guerry were supposed to have been taken "for safety," is not positively known, but it was on Ephraim Whistler's farm that Thomas Guerry was buried. Strangely though, John Tyson's grave never seems to have been sighted at Whistler's place, which was along the Chambersburg Pike west of Gettysburg. Therefore, the possibility remains that Guerry died enroute to a larger hospital and was merely dropped off at Whistler's for interment. But more likely is that both men ended up at Whistler's, with only Guerry's headboard surviving intact. This seems the most logical scenario, because Tyson's remains do not appear on any postwar shipments made to cemeteries in the South. The notation in Dr. O'Neal's journal lists Guerry, "—killed July 3; [and buried at] Whistlers in woods towards creek near [Jacob] Lott; right of Whistler's."

Why Private Guerry is sometimes mentioned as having been killed July 3, when earlier in the text Captain Patterson states that his battery was only in combat on July 2, is puzzling. The answer to this is still not clear, unless Company B did see action on both days, a fact Patterson did not remember. In viewing all the evidence, it does appear that Tom Guerry was mortally wounded on Friday, July 3. This last testimony may add credence to that assumption. It is a paragraph composed by his brother Dupont Guerry, of Macon, Georgia, and sent to the editor of *Confederate Veteran* magazine many years after the war:

> In the sixteenth year of his age [Thomas] determined that he would volunteer his services in defense of his country. His father and mother tried to dissuade him because of his extreme youth, saying that he would soon discover and regret his mistake; but he persisted and went to war the first opportunity, and was a model soldier for a year or more, until he lost his life at Gettysburg in his seventeenth year. He was in Cutt's Artillery, [Lane's during the campaign], and during the battle on the 3rd of July, 1863, while he was drawing the lanyard to fire his gun, an exploding shell from a battery of the enemy completely shattered his arm. His surgeon, Dr. Hill, amputated the limb at the shoulder and he sank under the operation, dying at one o'clock on the morning of July 4. When advised by Dr. Hill and others that death was very near, he was able to speak only a few words, and, addressing his captain, George M. Patterson, he said: "Tell my father and mother I am not sorry that I came to the war; that I fell at my post and died with my face to the enemy." His captain conveyed the message in a letter to his parents, and eyewitnesses to both occasions testified that he so fell and died.

It is true that the date of Guerry's wounding may be in some doubt, but fortunately, his pair of gravesites are not. In 1871 he was disinterred from the ground on Whistler's farm and sent with other Georgians to Savannah. There, on August 21, Thomas Guerry was buried for the last time in Laurel Grove Cemetery, Lot 854, Grave 13.

Still only a boy in age when a Yankee cannon ball cut short his life, Thomas was nevertheless, at his death, a grown man in heart and spirit. In his final hour, Private Guerry was posted by his country where he was needed the most, and exactly where he wanted to be.

IN LETTERS OF GOLD

Private George B. Powell,
Co. C, 14th Tennessee Infantry
Archer's Brigade, Heth's Division, Hill's Corps

Battlefields throughout our country should be preserved, if for no other reason than simply to honor the bravery, steadfastness, and dedication of Americans who faced, without complaint, the real possibility of death or disfigurement, for ideals and principles. Such ideals reach beyond the spectrum of normal human behavior, and lead to higher planes of existence.

Visitors to these battlefield parks can then explore the old places, and survey the terrain, the historic buildings, and even the monuments and cannons. Joined by guides, and rangers, and historians, these curious folks can take time to analyze and discuss and contemplate the men in the ranks, the generals in command, the weapons and tactics of war, and the cold facts of why, and where, and who. But in all this process and with its sincerity, the tourist can never, on these sites, experience many other essential intangibles: the taste, the smell, the sound, the feel of fear, and the ultimate knowledge of what it was like to be so close to death, in all its mystery and finality.

At the military park near Gettysburg, literally millions of people have tried to capture this essence of the soldier's ordeal. To do this, they often come to Cemetery Ridge. There the uninitiated stand and peer westward, and honestly try to imagine what it was like to move across an unending landscape of chaos and terror; of thundering cannon, flashing muskets, the air filled with innumerable fragments and lumps of iron and lead, all howling and tearing, and searching for the flesh and bone and blood that alone will satiate its terrible hunger. But for the present day visitor, that insight is unknowable, and so shall it remain.

However, for George B. Powell and other warriors like him, those intangibles were unlocked and explored long before. For on July 3, 1863, three-quarters of a mile from where multitudes would one day contemplate their deeds, Private Powell's brigade and six like it were poised to strike at the very epicenter of the enemy's stronghold. Before 4:00 p.m. on that long ago Friday, Powell's own regiment would be at the heart of the fiery vortex, with George Powell himself holding aloft the symbol of his presence there, his *raison d'etre*, as he came to know or not know, too soon, the ultimate secrets of creation.

A companion of George Powell's was there to record his friends last steps into eternity. His name was Sergeant Robert T. Mockbee, and he never forgot the scenes he witnessed on those fields of destruction, which, ironically, from that day forward, have remained peaceful and serene:

> [T]he Confederate infantry clad in somber homespun with nothing bright about them but their blood red battle flags and the glittering sheen of cold steel, moved out to that death charge as if on parade, under the eye of their great commander Genl Lee. Soon the cannon of the enemy opened sending shot and shell through the advancing lines, making wide gaps that was almost as soon closed by the sturdy veterans. The waving battle flags seemed to be the special mark. As soon as we came in range of the small arms, three men being shot with the colors of the Fourteenth Tenn, right before the "crest" at the stone fence was reached. The names of those three men deserve to appear in letters of gold in the most conspicuous place in the State House at Nashville. They were Thomas Davidson color bearer, (Co G), Col[u]mbus Horn color corporal (Co G) and [George] Powell (Co C) color corporal, who fell apparently dead just after crossing the Emmettsburg Pike, and within one hundred yards of the stone fence, from there it was carried by Borrey Smith of (Co F) to the stone fence from which the enemy fled, and at which place it was captured by the federals when they retook their lines, from which we had to flee before overpowering numbers.

It was not all Southern tribute that flattered the individual members of the 14th's color guard. The men who shot and killed George Powell and his companions were also impressed by the pluck and valor shown by their Confederate adversaries. One of these men, Sergeant Benjamin Hirst of the 14th Connecticut, who was standing behind the rock wall, remembered clearly a certain flag bearer from Tennessee, who could have been Powell:

> We must hold this Line to the Last man.... "Don't Fire until you get the order, and then fire Low and sure." It is the Clear Voice of Gen [John] Gibbon.... A few more words from Gen [Alexander] Hayes, and our own Gallant Col [Major T. G.] Ellis... runs along the Line[.] Ready, up with our Flags, Aim, Fire. And time it was too, for the Rebels seemed to me to be within 150 yards of us, just crossing the fences on the *Emmitsburg road*, and we could hear their Officers pressing them on to the charge. Fire, Fire, Fire, all along our Line.... The color bearer of the 14th Tennessee, with not a man of his regiment within a rod of him advanced steadily until he reached [a low rail fence in front of our regiment], when he rested his colors before him, then drew himself up to

his full h[e]ight, looking us calmly in the face. There he stood for several awful moments, when the sharp crack of two or three rifles fired simultaneously sent his brave soul to its maker.

The *shock of battle*, with living men turned into bloodied corpses, is when, in mere seconds, simple changes of great magnitude transform beings from life into non-life. But tragic death pales in comparison to the majesty of that color bearer. His bearing of pure sublime composure was greater than mortal panic and terror; it was, in fact, the defeat of death itself.

Many Confederates, including George Powell, were killed and buried in these fields on July 3. (gnmp)

HALLOWED BY THE BLOOD

Private Marcellus J. Wingfield,
Co. D, 1st Virginia Infantry
Kemper's Brigade, Pickett's Division, Longstreet's Corps

"I tell you," wrote Lieutenant John Dooley, on the evening of July 3, "there is no romance in making one of these charges.... [W]hen you rise to your feet as we did today, I tell you the enthusiasm of ardent breasts in many cases *ain't there....*"

Dooley, of the 1st Virginia, was speaking, of course, of the engagement at Gettysburg, and the attack he had just undertaken with part of General George Pickett's infantry division.

He and his companions had endured much on that unforgettable day. It started with a march to the field of battle, then a long wait in the open fields for the expected combat; and finally, almost two hours of enemy bombardment under a clear sky and a full summer sun. There, a number of his comrades were killed or injured by Yankee projectiles even before the main assault began. Some of his regiment fainted from the suffocating heat, while for others, the dread of what lay ahead sucked away their courage, and they too did not stand when all were ready to meet the foe.

But in the final moment, the majority of what was left of the "Old First" after two years of warfare, rose and formed ranks when Picket asked his commander the all important question: "General, shall I carry my men in?" After James Longstreet nodded a reply, a member of the 1st, 42-year-old Corporal Charles Loehr, claimed that only 160 Virginians lined up as the center regiment of Kemper's Brigade that day. Meanwhile, Loehr and fourteen others were thrown ahead as skirmishers, and the corporal said then he would not have given "twenty-five cents for his life if the charge was made."

It was a tense yet reflective time. Many of the Confederates were thinking of home, and one even noted humorously that they were also "looking for those men who can whip 10 Yankees to show up." Among the staunch veterans who did make the advance toward Cemetery Ridge was Private Howard M. Walthall of Company D. He, like most of his fellow Virginians, wondered, as they moved forward, "what we would do when the impact occurred." They did not have long to wait. According to Walthall, it happened quickly. The division was soon "cut to pieces...but by degrees."

Of the many and varied sights and sounds that Corporal Charles Loehr witnessed on that terrible afternoon, one small, almost meaningless event stood out in his mind for decades afterward. It concerned one of the regiment's rank and file, a private named Marcellus Wingfield, who accompanied Loehr as one of the unit's fifteen skirmishers. Wingfield must have been a good soldier. He had enlisted early, in August 1861 from Hanover County, but had experienced a rough two years prior to Lee's invasion of Pennsylvania. He was first wounded at Wynn's Mill, Virginia, in April 1862, and then was captured two months later at Frayser's Farm. Good luck then seemed to follow Wingfield after his release from a Union military prison in early August 1862, for nothing else shows up in his service file until July 1863. Since the last record simply reads, "Killed at Gettysburg," gratitude goes to a friend of Charles Loehr for a more revealing portrayal of Private Wingfield's final moments of existence. Quoting Loehr, the friend wrote:

> [Loehr said] that one of [his] comrades, M. J. Wingfield, called "Monk," turned to him when about half way across the field, saying,"Where are our re-inforcements?" On looking around nothing was in sight, except the three bri-

gades of Pickett about 300 yards in rear of our skirmish line and now subject to a storm of shells, tearing great gaps into the lines. [Loehr] then replied, "Monk, I don't see any," on which he replied, "We are going to be whipped, see if we don't." Alas for the poor fellow these were his last words, for a bullet ended his life only a few minutes afterward.

It is generally known that almost 100 percent of the Southern infantrymen who were shot to death in the Pickett-Pettigrew assault were interred as "unknowns" in trench burials on the ground where they died. Marcellus Wingfield was no exception, as so far nothing has come forth which proves otherwise. However, he and the other intrepid and unidentified Virginians were not totally forgotten. The next paragraph was written about them by a Confederate who fought with the 18th Virginia of Garnett's Brigade. It contains some powerful and thoughtful imagery, and could be proclaimed as their simple eulogy for the rest of time

> [All of] the killed and mortally wounded were left in Pennsylvania, and no one knows their graves, if buried. It may be that some of their bones may have been gathered into Hollywood, near Richmond, since the war. Who knows? Others, doubtless, have whitened and mingled into dust on the field where they fell, which now the plow-boy, whistling as he plows, turns over as common earth, unconscious that his plowshare is stirring sod hallowed by the blood of as brave men as the Continent has ever known.

Their sabers will not clank again
Their bayonets no more shine;
For them across the sunlit plain
Stretches no martial line;
For them her bloom sweet Nature yields
Upon their dewy bed.
And summer robs her dewy fields
To crown the Unknown Dead.

THEY'VE GOT TO GET MORE BLOOD

Private James L. Grissom,
Co. G, 7th Tennessee Infantry
Archer's Brigade, Heth's Division, Hill's Corps

Thirty-seven years had passed since a wounded Captain Fergus S. Harris, using two discarded muskets for crutches, came stumbling back across the shot-torn fields of "Pickett's Charge." It was the summer of 1899, and Harris was on a tour of the Gettysburg battleground accompanied by the commissioners who oversaw the new government park. As the group stopped their carriage along Seminary Ridge near Spangler's Woods, Captain Harris and his fellow travelers began the nearly one mile trek to Cemetery Ridge, for Harris wished "to walk, as far as possible, over the very ground upon which we walked that fatal day." The fatal day, of course, was July 3, when Archer's depleted little brigade of Alabama and Tennessee infantrymen, fighting on the left of Pickett's Division, cooperated in Longstreet's thrust at the Union line.

While standing there, Harris said he became almost oblivious to his current surroundings, and began to imagine again all of the sights and sounds of battle experienced so long ago. He remembered the men of his beloved 7th Tennessee returning from the disastrous charge—himself on crutches watching General Lee endeavoring to rally the broken Confederate regiments, and finally, how Lt. Col. Samuel Shepard later reformed the 7th for muster, and only thirteen men were left to stand in the ranks.

But Captain Harris relived something else that day in 1899. In 1863 he had witnessed the last moments of James L. Grissom, and that death came back to him forcefully as he glanced at the historic land around him. Harris had not personally known Grissom's real name, as they were in different companies, but he knew his regimental nickname, the "Black Ram."

The first memory that came flooding back was of himself and several of his men lying under the Federal guns, "side by side on Cemetery crest, with a perfect shower of shot, shell and ball" flying over them. According to the captain, someone suggested, "lets surrender." When that was proposed, reported Harris, "Brave Tom Holloway raised his head and said, 'Let's never surrender.' Just then a bullet went crashing through his brain." Harris then remembered Grissom, the "Black Ram," who was part of the group, taking cover. When the "Ram" was asked if it would be better to surrender, he replied, "They've got to get more blood out of me than they have before I ever surrender."

Later, as the survivors of the charge started for the rear, the "Ram" was severely wounded before he had gone twenty steps. But that did not stop him from assisting Captain Robert Miller back toward Seminary Ridge. However, their bitter retreat, observed Harris, sealed the fate of James Grissom. As they made their way rearward, enemy artillery shells continued to make the journey a hazardous undertaking. In one instance a particularly loud projectile came screaming toward them. The "Black Ram" dropped Captain Miller and jumped ten feet to his left aiming to take cover behind the stump of a large tree, just recently cut. He did not make it. Just as the "Ram" stooped, wrote Captain Harris, "the shell struck him on the shoulder and seem[ed] to have exploded about the same time. It literally tore him into a thousand pieces and dug a great hole into the ground."

Standing there on the same spot thirty-seven years later, Harris wanted to find the old stump. He looked around and soon saw that the remnants of it were still there, but what was left was only a small chunk of rotten wood. It was enough of a landmark though, and enabled the "Black Ram's" tragic story to come to a curious close. The captain himself finishes the tale through the words of an article he wrote for his hometown newspaper, when he returned from Gettysburg in 1899:

> This field is now in corn, and while I was relating this circumstance to the commissioners, a man who was ploughing the corn was standing there listening, and he said "I will get you a piece of the shell that killed the "Black Ram.'" He drove his long keen bull-tongue into the ground deeper than it has ever been ploughed before, and when in the exact spot[,] brought to the surface a piece of the shell [that] I am certain is the piece that killed the "Black Ram." I have brought the relic home with me and now have it.

Captain Harris eventually learned that the "Black Ram" was Jim Grissom, whose "people" he said, "yet live in Wilson County." That knowledge led Harris to this conclusion: "If they will take this relic and take care of it as a momento of one of the finest of America's soldiers, and of the battlefield of Gettysburg, I will give it to them."

IN A JUST & NOBLE CAUSE

Captain Edward F. Satterfield,
Co. H, 55th North Carolina Infantry
Davis' Brigade, Heth's Division, Hill's Corps

The contest of words between Virginia and North Carolina as to "who went the farthest at Gettysburg," (meaning, of course, who had done the most fighting), began subtly even before the year 1863 had ended. But following the Civil War, the arguments intensified, until it was hard to believe that the two states had fought on the same side. The crux of the problem was this: soldiers from North Carolina believed their reputation had been sullied by statements from the Virginians, that they would have succeeded in Lee's final attack on July 3, had the troops on General Pickett's left, many of whom were from the Old North State, not given way and retreated. This discussion still goes on. The following story examines the role of one of the participants in that great drama, now past.

That person was E. Fletcher Satterfield, a 24-year-old lawyer and resident of Roxboro, and a graduate of the University of North Carolina. By November 1861, Satterfield had enlisted into the 14th North Carolina Volunteers. But before a year had passed, he was appointed 1st lieutenant of

Company H, 55th regiment, and by the following March, captain. However, it was in the hours of the Battle of Gettysburg, and during the very climax of the "Pickett-Pettigrew Charge," that Captain Satterfield attained immortality. For no matter how long Virginia and North Carolina disagreed on which state had sacrificed more in its country's fight for independence, one fact was certain: Captain E. F. Satterfield had done his whole duty that day, a point no man could ever criticize.

The supreme accomplishment of Captain Satterfield, and his sad demise, can best be described by a comrade who was near his side at the time. He was Sergeant J. Augustus Whitley of Company E:

> As to the [third] day's fight at Gettysburg, our regiment...was a part of the first line. We were supported by the second and third lines. We charged across the field and crossed a road about one hundred yards from the federal works (a stone fence). Our line was cut down to a mere skirmish line when we got to the works, about thirty feet on the right of that old barn. Our flag had fallen a few yards back. The Yankees had run back to a second stone fence, a hundred or more yards. There was not a Yankee to be seen. We had whipped and repulsed them at this point. I looked back for our support and saw them in full retreat, at least 150 yards from me. Captain Satterfield was the only man I saw near me on my left. He and I started a few paces back, when a shell from our batteries that were protecting the retreat of the second and third lines fell just in front of him, exploded and literally tore him to pieces. I fell behind a small elm, and was soon ordered to surrender.

Another soldier who was in the vicinity of Whitley and Satterfield, was 3rd Lieutenant Thomas D. Falls of Company C. In a letter written in 1896 to Alfred Belo, the 55th's former lieutenant colonel, Falls related how Captain Satterfield was leading "a portion of the regiment," when he "fell within nine yards of the enemy's stone wall with colors in hand." Belo himself said that the three men, Falls, Whitley, and Satterfield, "reached the extreme point of the Confederate advance on that fatal day." This spot, he claimed, was eighty yards to the left and *beyond* where General Armistead of Virginia had been stopped.

Possibly the most tragic footnote of all is that Capt. Satterfield, killed by "friendly" artillery at the very pinnacle of his military career, almost did not arrive in time to meet the death that awaited him. Just a few days prior to that moment, he was returning on foot from a sick furlough, trying his best to rejoin the army, already in or moving toward Pennsylvania. When he reached Winchester on June 27, Satterfield took a few minutes to compose a quick note to his mother. In it he declared he had already walked "between 90 & 100 miles" but was still unsure of the location of the brigade. Satterfield ended by saying, "I am very well but my feet are very sore."

Capt Satterfield would have believed he died
in "a just & noble cause."

(sch)

The captain finally reached his unit, but only after it had been engaged with the Union army on July 1. According to Private J. D. Williams, when Satterfield arrived, he expressed sorrow at the condition of his company, and also that he had not been present to lead them into battle. Williams added that the captain "bursted into tears" believing that some of his men hated him for being absent.

Lieutenant William Wayne Davis of Company H, in writing to the captain's sister Sue Satterfield on August 10, commented how "I was told at the regiment that my poor friend had a strong presentiment that he would be killed...he told his friends & had a long talk with a Williams of the Regiment belonging to his Company who is one of the best Christians I ever saw...." J. D. Williams must not have heard of the aforementioned presentiment, for on another occasion he said to Sue Satterfield, "I never heard him say anything about falling on the battlefield...." A second officer wrote to Sue on September 19. He was Lieutenant William Hunt Townes of Company D. Townes called Satterfield, "my intimate personal friend whom I loved as a brother & whose loss, in common with all officers of this Regt., I most sincerely mourn. His family will have the proud consolation of knowing that he fell at his post doing [his] duty—& left an improachable & unsullied name...." Similarly, a classmate, R. C. Pearson, Jr., of Morgantown, NC, sent a letter to the captain's father, Green D. Satterfield, on August 5:

> Sir, In looking over the account of the late Battles in Penna I was deeply grieved to see among the names of our thousands of departed Heroes was recorded that of my dearest friend your son Ed Fletcher Satterfield.... [We were] chums while at College, the friendship then engendered had in manhood's life ripened into filial affection. He was kind & generous to a fault, Noble & Brave[,] as testimony of this he gave up his life in a just & noble cause....

But perhaps the most intriguing words relating to the story of Captain Satterfield had been jotted down, in playfulness, over a year earlier by his friend, Jennie Pearson. She was the younger sister of the gentleman quoted above, and since his student days at Chapel Hill, Fletcher Satterfield had kept up a correspondence with her. On this occasion, and well before the 55th North Carolina participated in combat with an enemy force, Jennie made an unusual and prophetic statement. In that letter to Fletcher she said: "I hope if you get in a fight, Lieut. Satterfield will make his 'mark' & in that a good many Yankees are killed."

In the captain's last moments at Gettysburg, Jennie's words were curiously, and most emphatically, fulfilled.

Captain Isaac D. Stamps
(story on page 84)

THE END

Oh! choose ye a place where the dead may rest,
And gather their bones from the field.
On their nameless graves let the sod be press'd,
For Death has their mission sealed.
Yes, choose ye a spot where the dead may sleep,
Nor storms their bones discover,
A spot where their lov'd ones may come and weep,
"When this cruel war is over."

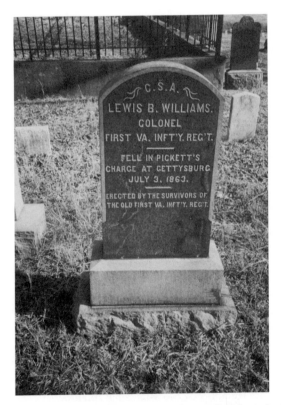

Very few of Gettysburg's Confederate dead were honored with a private burial and a beautiful headstone, similiar to this grave in Hollywood Cemetery. (twh)

SOURCES

The major sources found in this book for the fifty Confederates "killed in action," or who died of wounds received at Gettysburg, are catalogued below. In many of the book's described accounts, the names of Drs. John W. C. O'Neal and Rufus B. Weaver are referenced for miscellaneous "burial lists" they completed between 1863 and 1873. Since those rosters are not indicated in each instance where utilized, they are hereby acknowledged to be compilations developed from the originals by the Chief Historian at the Gettysburg National Military Park, (GNMP), Kathleen George Harrison.

There were, of course, other general sources employed to complete this project, such as Robert K. Krick's "Gettysburg Death Roster," as well as many other common and easily found reference works. These were not cited, as they served as "background" only, and not as the core material for this book.

Preface and Acknowledgements
J. T. Trowbridge, "The Field of Gettysburg," *Atlantic Monthly*, Vol. 16, (Nov. 1865), 618.
S. E. Bucklin, *In Hospital and Camp* (Philadelphia, PA: 1869), 191.
Timothy Foote, Quote in the *Smithsonian* (Washington, D.C.: Dec. 1999), 40.
Introduction
H. R. Garden, captain, Garden's "Palmetto" Battery. From a letter written to the Sumter (South Carolina) *Herald*, and printed on Aug. 29, 1902.
C. W. Clark, "I Resolve To Fight," Unpublished paper drawn from the original letters of Thomas G. Clark and sons in the "Mississippi Room" of the library of the University of Mississippi, University, MS: 2000, 1-11.
The Gettysburg (Pennsylvania) *Compiler*, A newspaper "Notice" printed on May 29, 1888.
Gettysburg's *Star and Sentinel*, on the same date, ran a similar "headboard" story, but that paper gave a slightly different version of events. An attempt to identify the actual name of "Mrs. Clayton Hoke" turned up nothing in the Adams County Historical Society.
S. W. Sylvia & M. J. O'Donnell, *The Illustrated History of American Civil War Relics* (Orange, VA: 1978), 112-113.
A. T. Roane, "Civil War—A Relic of Liberty," [sic] An unpuplished paper written by the nephew of Captain Thomas Clark, courtesy of Charlie W. Clark, Bruce, MS, n.d., [circa 1890s], 1.
A. J. Ryan, "The Deathless Dead," *Confederate Veteran* (Nashville, TN: 1893-1932), Vol. 8, 504.
Note: In a recent book on Davis' Brigade by T. P. Williams, (p. 102), the author states that he believes that both sons of Thomas Clark were killed on July 3.

July 1, 1863
Corporal Charles Humphreys, 2nd Mississippi Infantry
S. W. Hankins, *The Simple Story of a Soldier*, Nashville, TN: 1912, 40-50.
Private Benjamin Stone, Page's Virginia Battery
The War of the Rebellion: A Compilation of the Official Records of the Union and Confederate Armies, 128 vols. in 4 series, Vol. 27, Pt. 2 (Washington, D.C.: U. S. Government Printing Office, 1880-1901), 458 & 603. Hereafter cited as *OR*.

Confederate Veteran, Vol. 8, 25.

Captain Campbell Iredell, 47th North Carolina Infantry
L. G. Young, "Northern Prison Life," *The Land We Love* (Charlotte, NC: Nov.-Apr., 1866-1867), 13-14.

Unknown Georgia Captain
Sister M. D. Salomon, Deceased Sisters, Archives of St. Joseph's College, 1932, 106
C. P. Cole, Article in the Courtland (New York) *Gazette and Banner*, July 16, 1863.

Captain William Ousby, 43rd North Carolina Infantry
Bucklin, 166 & 189.
Trowbridge, 618.
J. L. Ousby, Unpublished letters in the "Southern Historical Collection," Univ. of North Carolina, Chapel Hill, NC.
There were approximately 5,500 Confederate soldiers killed and mortally wounded at Gettysburg. Of this number, less than 1,200 were found with *identified* graves on or near the battlefield.

Corporal Leonidas Torrence, 23rd North Carolina Infantry
The North Carolina Historical Review (Raleigh, NC: Dept. of Archives and History, Oct. 1959), 514-517.
H. Monroe, ed., "The Road to Gettysburg," *Southern Historical Society Papers*, Vol. 7 (Richmond, VA), 351.

Private J. R. Stewart, 23rd North Carolina Infantry
O. W. Blacknall, Unpublished biography of Maj. C. C. Blacknall, Dept. of Archives and History (Raleigh, NC: n.d., post-1900), 27-32.
J. F. Coghill, Letters written from Williamsport, MD, and Rockville, VA, July 9 & 10, 1863, in the "Southern Historical Collection," Univ. of North Carolina, Chapel Hill, NC.
As an example, during the war North Carolina furnished to the Confederacy 102,000 men. Of these 14,522 were killed. Virginia, on the other hand, sent 128,000 to the Southern army, but only 5,328 of that number died in battle.

Captain William Cromer, 13th South Carolina Infantry
J. A. Walker, Article in the Philadelphia *Times*, Mar. 17, 1883.
J. F. J. Caldwell, *The History of a Brigade of South Carolinians* (Philadelphia, PA: 1866), 144.
S. G. Welch, *A Confederate Surgeon's Letters to His Wife* (Marietta, GA: 1954), 59.

July 2, 1863

Private Joseph Love, 5th Texas Infantry
J. E. Love, Medical record, Case # 1592, National Museum of Health and Medicine, Armed Forces Institute of Pathology, Washington, D.C.
Loudon Park Cemetery, Cemetery Register, Row B, Grave # 77, Baltimore, MD.
Confederate Veteran, Vol. 15, 364-365.

Captain James Ellison, 15th Alabama Infantry
W. C. Oates, *The War Between The Union And The Confederacy* (Dayton, OH: 1974), 227 & 613.

Privates G. A. & W. C. Jones, 5th Texas Infantry
J. W. Stevens, *Reminiscences of the Civil War* (Hillsboro, TX: 1902), 114.
T. C. Harbaugh, "The Unknown Dead," *Confederate Veteran*, Vol. 10, 263.

Sergeant John Moseley, 4th Alabama Infantry
W. C. Ward, "How John W. Moseley Died on the Field of Gettysburg," Article in the "Maj. W. M. Robbins Papers," (c. 1898), in the GNMP Library.

W. C. Ward, "Incidents and Personal Experiences on the Battlefield of Gettysburg," *Confederate Veteran*, Vol. 8, 345.

Confederate Veteran, Vol. 8, 405.

A. M. Judson, *History of the Eighty-Third Pennsylvania Volunteers, 1861-1865* (Erie, PA) 134-135.

The letter of John Moseley has been reprinted in several different sources, and it appears that some slight changes were made in each instance. Therefore, it is impossible to give the exact transcription.

Lt. Colonel Benjamin Carter, 4th Texas Infantry

Article in the Adams *Sentinel* (Gettysburg, PA), Aug. 4, 1863.

Confederate Veteran, Vol. 25, 556.

J. C. West, *A Texan In Search Of A Fight* (Waco, TX: 1969), 102.

Jacob Hoke, *The Great Invasion* (Dayton, OH: 1887), 496.

A. K. McClure, "Old Time Notes of Pennsylvania," (Philadelphia, PA: 1905), 105-107. A 71-year-old physician named Jeremiah Senseney was mentioned as the doctor in charge of the Chambersburg hospitals; the name was also noted as being Abraham H. Senseny.

Captain William Dunklin, 44th Alabama Infantry

J. L. Smith, *History of the Corn Exchange Regiment* (Philadelphia, PA: 1888), 261-262.

J. G. Acken, ed., *Inside the Army of the Potomac* (Mechanicsburg, PA: 1998), 310-311.

Corporal Samuel Thompson, Dement's Maryland Battery

W. W. Goldsborough, *The Maryland Line in the Confederate Army* (Baltimore, MD: 1900), 265 & 267.

J. W. F. Hatton, Unpublished memoir in the Library of Congress, Washington, D.C., DLC # 9243, (July 2, 1863), 452-453.

Private Rufus Franks, 4th Alabama Infantry

J. D. Stocker, ed., *From Huntsville to Appomattox* (Knoxville, TN: 1996), 109, 208 & 255-256.

Lieutenant Jesse Person, 1st North Carolina Cavalry

P. M. Shevchuk, "The Battle of Hunterstown," *Gettysburg Magazine* (Dayton, OH: Issue #1, July 1989), 93.

C. J. Iredell, Letter dated July 7, 1863, to Robert J. Shaw, in the collections of Perkins Library, Duke University, Durham, NC.

Unknown Negro

Article in the New York *Herald*, July 11, 1863.

Maine at Gettysburg (Portland, ME: 1898), 526.

In original papers, the name was James Chodman or Chadman.

E. B. Henderson, *Plantation Echoes* (Columbus, OH: 1904), 59.

Private Samuel Watson, 5th Texas Infantry

E. F. Conklin, *Women at Gettysburg* (Gettysburg, PA: Thomas Publications,1993), 352-354.

E. M. Goldsborough, Letter dated Sept. 22, 1863, to Harriet Watson of Washington, TX, in files of the GNMP Library.

Private Jackson Giles, 9th Georgia Infantry

George Hillyer, "Battle of Gettysburg," An address to the Walton County, GA, Confederate Veterans, in the Walton (Georgia) *Tribune*, Aug. 2, 1904, 5.

The chaplain in this story was probably William Flynn, 16th Georgia Infantry.

Major Donald McLeod, 8th South Carolina Infantry

Hoke, 595-497.

OR, Vol. 27, Pt. 2, 369.

D. A. Dickert, *History of Kershaw's Brigade* (Dayton, OH: 1973), 251.

Captain C. M. Ballard, 8th Georgia Infantry

J. R. Lane, An address printed in the Chatham County (North Carolina) *Record*, on Aug. 14, 1890.

Walter Clark, *Histories of the Several Regiments and Battalions from North Carolina*, Vol. 2 (Goldsboro, NC: 1901), 369.

John Rozier, *The Granite Farm Letters* (Athens, GA: 1988), 115-116.

Lt. Colonel Francis Kearse, 50th Georgia Infantry

J. H. Wert, *A Complete Handbook of the Monuments and Indications...on the Gettysburg Battlefield* (Harrisburg, PA: 1886), 109.

A. M. Emory, Unpublished diary, August 1863, in the GNMP Library.

G. W. Rose, "Location of Confederate Graves in the Vicinity of the Rose House," unpublished notebook in the GNMP Library, n.d.

Keith Bohannon, ed., "Wounded & Captured at Gettysburg," *Military Images*, May-Jun. 1988, 14.

Constance Pendelton, ed., *Confederate Memoirs* (Bryn Athyn, PA: 1958), 34-36.

There was no "Sgt. Hersey" of the 50th Georgia killed at Gettysburg.

F. L. Riley, ed., W. A. Love, "Mississippi at Gettysburg," *Mississippi Historical Society Magazine*, Vol. 9 (Oxford, MS: 1906), 41.

Sargeant Travis Maxey, 8th Georgia Infantry

J. C. Reid, An unpublished memoir in the collections of the Alabama Dept. of Archives and History (Montgomery, AL: n.d.), 69-72.

Private James Ouzts, 14th South Carolina Infantry

J. L. Johnson, *The University Memorial*, Univ. of Virginia (Baltimore, MD: 1871), 457-464.

D. A. & A. S. Tompkins, *Company K—Fourteenth South Carolina Volunteers* (Charlotte, NC: 1897), 20-21.

W. C. Burbage, "Re-Interment of the South Carolina Dead from Gettysburg," *United Daughters of the Confederacy Magazine*, Vol. 8 (June 1989), 15-16.

J. F. J. Caldwell, 146.

There was some discrepancy as to when Capt. Haskell was killed. One source puts it on July 3, others on July 2 after 6 p.m. Most reports say July 2, but do not give a precise time. Likewise, there is some question about Pvt. Ouzts' age. R. K. Krick says 23, his military records, 19.

Lieutenant Frederick Bliss, 8th Georgia Infantry

Hillyer, 3-4.

M. P. Joslyn, ed., *Charlotte's Boys* (Berryville, VA: 1996), 159-161, 179, 304-305, 307, 310 & 336.

Private Archibald Duke, 17th Mississippi Infantry

J. W. Duke. "Mississippians at Gettysburg," *Confederate Veteran*, Vol. 14, 216.

Private William Booton, 8th Georgia Infantry

M. B. Sherbley. "Membership Record of...Being a brief history of the military career of her uncle, William Sinclair Booton. Co. A. 8th Ga. Regt." n.d., (c. 1924), 7-11.

This poem is inscribed over the graves of the Confederate Dead in Oakland Cemetery, Gaffney, SC.

Lieutenant John Caldwell, 33rd North Carolina Infantry

An article printed in the Gettysburg *Compiler*, Feb. 7, 1888, concerning "a recent letter from Raleigh, N.C. to the St. Louis *Democrat*," about John, the son of Tod R. Caldwell.

C. M. Avery, Letter dated July 18, 1863, at Bunker Hill, VA, to Tod R. Caldwell. "Caldwell Papers," # 128, "Southern Historical Collection," Univ. of North Carolina, Chapel Hill, NC.

(Mrs.) C. A. Elher, *The Patriot Daughters of Lancaster, Hospital Scenes After the Battle of Gettysburg* (Philadelphia, PA: 1864), 20.

W. H. Lucas, Letter to J. B. Neathery, Esq. Dec. 9, 1887, from Middleton, NC, in the GNMP Library.

Lt. Colonel John Mounger, 9th Georgia Infantry
OR, Vol. 27, Pt. 2, 399-400 & 775.

Mounger Family Letters, "9th Georgia File," in the GNMP Library.

Captain Isaac Stamps, 21st Mississippi Infantry
T. J. Winschel, "To Assuage the Grief," *Gettysburg Magazine*, Issue # 7 (Dayton, OH: July 1992), 77-82.

In November 1863, the body of Captain Samuel W. Gray, 57th N. C., was recovered by his father and taken back to his home state.

Private John Dixon, 3rd Georgia Infantry
An article in the Gettysburg *Compiler*, Aug. 9, 1884.

G. A. Coco, *On the Bloodstained Field II* (Gettysburg, PA: Thomas Publications, 1989), 47.

OR, Vol. 27, Pt. 2, 627-628.

Private Robert Crawford, 11th Alabama Infantry
F. W. Thompson, Letter to his sister and mother from, "Camp near Bunker Hill, Va," July 17, 1863, in the "11th Alabama File," GNMP Library.

July 3, 1863

Private Whiting Hockman, 10th Virginia Infantry
Jacob Hoke, *Historical Reminiscences of the War...* (Chambersburg, PA: 1884), 195.

Sergeant William Prince, 5th Virginia Infantry
Lawrence Wilson, "Charge Up Culp's Hill," An article in the Washington (D.C.) Post, July 9, 1899, 22.

D. A. Dickert, 134.

G. K. Collins, *Memoirs of the 149th Regiment New York Volunteer Infantry* (Hamilton, NY: 1995), 148-149.

J. H. Wert, 201.

Private James Larew, 1st Virginia Cavalry
B. J. Haden, *Reminiscences of J. E. B. Stuart's Cavalry* (Charlottesville, VA: 190?), 24-25.

A. C. Gordon, "The Confederate Dead," *Southern Historical Society Papers*, Vol. 25, 382.

Private John Hite, 33rd Virginia Infantry
H. P. Jessup, ed., *The Painful News I have To Write* (Baltimore, MD: 1998),143, 146-147 & 148-149.

H. K. Douglas, *I Rode With Stonewall* (Chapel Hill, NC: 1968), 252-253.

A. C. Gordon, 383.

Captain William Murray, 1st Maryland Battalion
G. W. Booth, *Personal Reminiscences of a Maryland Soldier....* (Baltimore, MD: 1898), 79.

R. H. McKim, "The 2nd Maryland Infantry," An oration delivered on May 7, 1909, 8. A copy is in the GNMP Library.

D. C. Toomey, *Marylanders at Gettysburg* (Baltimore, MD: 1994), 23-25 & 44.

R. H. McKim, *A Soldier's Recollections* (Washington, D.C.: 1983), 205.

J. W. Thomas, Unpublished memoir in the "1st Maryland, C.S.A. File," GNMP Library.

"The Gallant Dead," An article in the Baltimore *Telegram*, c.1879, author unknown, n.p. See the "1st Maryland C.S.A. File," GNMP Library.

Lieutenant Daniel Featherston, 11th Mississippi Infantry

S. H. Stubbs, *Duty—Honor—Valor* (Philadelphia, MS: 2000), 421 & 775.

Henderson, 59.

Sergeant Joseph Lynn, 8th Virginia Infantry

R. A. Shotwell, "Virginia and North Carolina in the Battle of Gettysburg," *Our Living and Our Dead*, Vol. 4 (Mar.-Aug., 1876), 89.

Norborne Berkeley, "Gettysburg," Unpublished memoir in the "8th Virginia File," GNMP Library, n.p., n.d.

Captain James Kincaid, 52nd North Carolina Infantry

Alexander McNeil, Letter to David G. Porter, Aug. 16, 1863, from "Bristowburg, VA," in the "14th Connecticut File," GNMP Library.

"List of Confederate Wounded in the U. S. General Hospital, George Wolf Farm." National Archives, Washington, D.C., RG 94, 9W3, Row 8, Book 2.

Captain William Bissell, 8th Virginia Infantry

Margaret Bissell, Unpublished memoir written from Bel-Air, VA, July 22, 1863, in the "8th Virginia File," GNMP Library.

Private William McCulloch, 14th Tennessee Infantry

Junius Kimble, "W. H. McCulloch," Unpublished memoir written in Eastland, TX, n.d., n.p., in the files of the GNMP Library.

Confederate Veteran, Vol. 15, 80.

Lieutenant Wesley Battle, 37th North Carolina Infantry

OR, Vol. 27, Pt. 2, 666.

Kenneth Hickey, Letter to W. L. Battle, Apr. 16, (?), in the "37th North Carolina File," GNMP Library.

There is no record that Lt. Battle had a brother killed at South Mountain, MD. Perhaps Hickey got this information from another Confederate he assisted on July 3.

Corporal Columbus Cook, 11th Mississippi Infantry

S. H. Stubbs, *For My Children* (Privately printed, possibily at Philadelphia, MS: 1993), 100-101 & 289-190.

Private Thomas Guerry, Sumter Georgia Artillery

OR, Vol. 27, Pt. 2, 635-636.

F. R. Galloway, "Gettysburg—The Battle and Retreat," *Confederate Veteran*, Vol. 21, 388.

Dupont Guerry, "Gallant Thomas Legrande Guerry," *Confederate Veteran*, Vol. 22, 103.

Private George Powell, 14th Tennessee Infantry

R. T. Mockbee, "Historical Sketch of the 14th Tennessee Regiment of Infantry, C.S.A., 1861-1865," n.d, n.p., in the files of the GNMP Library.

R. L. Bee, ed., *The Boys From Rockville* (Knoxville, TN: 1998), 150.

Borrey Smith was also known as "Boney," and according to some sources, may have been a black freedman or a slave who fought with the Tennesseans.

Private Marcellus Wingfield, 1st Virginia Infantry

J. T. Durkin, ed., *John Dooley, Confederate Soldier, His War Journal* (Notre Dame, IN: 1963), 104-105.

Confederate Veteran, Vol. 12, 519.

B. R. Kinney, Quote in the memoir, "12th North Carolina at Gettysburg." n.p, n.d., in the files at the GNMP Library.

H. M. Walthall, Unpublished memoir in the "1st Virginia File," GNMP Library.

C. T. Loehr, "The 'Old First' Virginia at Gettysburg," *Southern Historical Society Papers*, Vol. 32, 33-40.

Richard Irby, *Historical Sketch of the Nottoway Grays...* (Richmond, VA: 1878), 29.

Harbaugh, 264.

Private James Grissom, 7th Tennessee Infantry

F. S. Harris, "From Gettysburg," An article in the Lebanon (Tennessee) *Democrat*, on Aug. 10, 1899, n.p.

A. C. Gordon, 384.

Captain Edward Satterfield, 55th North Carolina Infantry

J. A. Whitley, Letter printed in the Galveston (Texas) *Daily News*, on June 21, 1896.

T. D. Falls, Letter written to Lt. Col. A. H. Belo on June 1, 1896, and printed in the Galveston (Texas) *Daily News* on June 21, 1896.

A. H. Belo, "The Battle of Gettysburg," An article in the Dallas (Texas) *Morning News*, Feb. 24, 1900.

E. F. Satterfield, Unpublished letter to his mother dated June 27, 1863, from Winchester, VA, in the private collection of Dr. Michael Masters, Clyde, NC.

Sam and Wes Small, *The Horse Soldier Catalogue* #11 (Gettysburg, PA: Fall 1990, 27-30.

"A. S. M," Untitled poem, printed in the Adams *Sentinel* (Gettysburg, PA: Mar. 15, 1864), 1.

PHOTO CREDITS

OTHER BOOKS BY GREG COCO

On the Bloodstained Field
On the Bloodstained Field II
War Stories
Killed In Action
A Vast Sea of Misery
A Strange and Blighted Land
From Ball's Bluff to Gettysburg and Beyond
The Civil War Infantryman
A Concise Guide to the Artillery at Gettysburg
Rebel Humor

THOMAS PUBLICATIONS publishes books about the American Colonial era, the Revolutionary War, the Civil War, and other important topics. For a complete list of titles, please visit our web site at:

http://thomaspublications.com

Or write to:

THOMAS PUBLICATIONS
P.O. Box 3031
Gettysburg, PA 17325